Eternal in Love

Studies in the Doctrine of God: Exploring Classical and Relational Theism

Studies in the Doctrine of God: Exploring Classical and Relational Theism is a series of books that explore the nature and attributes of God in the context of current debates over classical theism and relational models of God. This series includes volumes that advance the discussion of the doctrine of God, with particular focus on advancing the discussion of conceptions of God that affirm the Creator-creature distinction while also affirming that God is freely and genuinely related to the world in a way that makes a difference to God. Such conceptions of God are sometimes referred to as modified or moderate classical theism or neoclassical theism. These conceptions of God are classical in that they affirm some core tenets of classical theism (divine perfection, necessity, aseity, self-sufficiency, unity, eternity, immutability, omnipotence, omniscience with foreknowledge, and omnipresence). At the same time, such conceptions are also relational in that they affirm God is genuinely related to the world and depart from one or more attributes of (strict) classical theism such as divine timelessness, strict simplicity, strict immutability, and/or strict impassibility. Each volume in this series will address some aspect or aspects of the nature and attributes of God and the God-world relation in a way that advances the discussion of approaches that are both classical and relational in these respects.

SERIES EDITORS:
R. T. Mullins
John C. Peckham

EDITORIAL BOARD:
David Baggett
Daniel Castelo
Paul Copan
Jeanine Diller
Scott Harrower
William Hasker
Veli-Matti Kärkkäinen
Kevin Kinghorn
Andrew Loke
Roger Olson
Anastasia Scrutton
Jordan Wessling

Eternal in Love

A Little Book About a Big God

R. T. MULLINS

CASCADE *Books* • Eugene, Oregon

ETERNAL IN LOVE
A Little Book About a Big God
Studies in the Doctrine of God

Copyright © 2024 R. T. Mullins. All rights reserved. Except for brief quotations in critical publications or reviews, no part of this book may be reproduced in any manner without prior written permission from the publisher. Write: Permissions, Wipf and Stock Publishers, 199 W. 8th Ave., Suite 3, Eugene, OR 97401.

Cascade Books
An Imprint of Wipf and Stock Publishers
199 W. 8th Ave., Suite 3
Eugene, OR 97401

www.wipfandstock.com

PAPERBACK ISBN: 978-1-6667-3097-5
HARDCOVER ISBN: 978-1-6667-2298-7
EBOOK ISBN: 978-1-6667-2299-4

Cataloguing-in-Publication data:

Names: Mullins, R. T.

Title: Eternal in love : a little book about a big god / R. T. Mullins.

Description: Eugene, OR : Cascade Books, 2024 | Series: Studies in the Doctrine of God | Includes bibliographical references and index.

Identifiers: ISBN 978-1-6667-3097-5 (paperback) | ISBN 978-1-6667-2298-7 (hardcover) | ISBN 978-1-6667-2299-4 (ebook)

Subjects: LCSH: God. | Theology, Doctrinal.

Classification: BT75 .M84 2024 (paperback) | BT75 .M84 (ebook)

VERSION NUMBER 082324

For those chasing eternity

Contents

Acknowledgments | ix

Preface | xi

1 What Is God? | 1
2 The Essential Attributes of God | 15
3 The Eternal God Without Creation | 34
4 The Consequences of Creation | 54
5 Why Create Anything at All? | 69
6 What Are God's Creative Options? | 84
7 Why Create Any Particular Universe? | 98
8 The Problem of Foreknowledge and Passibility | 129

Conclusion | 144

Bibliography | 147

Acknowledgments

THERE ARE MANY PEOPLE to thank that have contributed to the completion of this book. I am grateful to Ryan Shields, Megan Martin, Alan Rhoda, Arjuna Gallagher, Than Christopoulos, Brandon Christian Sullivan, Tyler Henry, James Gibson, Dennis Fuller, David Thurman, Lucas Curcio, and Dustin Burlet for reading an earlier draft of this manuscript. Their feedback was invaluable. Special thanks to Thomas Jay Oord for encouraging me to write a book that would be more accessible and affordable than the average academic book.

Much gratitude is offered to my 2023 Palm Beach Atlantic University class on God, Time, and Creation. As I worked through some of the material of this book with the masters' students, their enthusiasm and probing questions encouraged me to keep on track with completing this book. Joseph Bradley, Zackary Kralik, Andrew Mercantini, Lucas Merritt, Matthew Mittelberg, Micah Neighbors, Giovanni Pantaleo, Elli Patterson, Matthew Pique, Anna Ruth, and Travis Satterfield. Special mention must go to Andrew Drinkard for his feedback during class, and his masterful editing skills. Without his editorial work on this manuscript, this book would not have been completed on time.

Thanks to New Brunswick Church of Christ for inviting me to preach in December of 2021. My sermon on friendship with God formed the basis for the preface to this book. Thanks to my family Tom, Jan, and Kelli Mullins for their support during this time.

I would be remiss if I did not mention the Helsinki Collegium for Advanced Study. My research fellowship during 2020–2022 allowed me the opportunity to publish many articles, complete one book manuscript, and write up a majority of the book that stands before you.

Appreciation is due to Tyler McNabb and Mike DeVito for pushing me to finally write up my reflections on the problem of divine foreknowledge and passibility. Also, much gratitude for the Berlin Religion and Emotion cohort. I presented an earlier draft of my work on the problem of foreknowledge and passibility, and their feedback was incredibly helpful. Thanks also to the Philadelphia Philosophy of Religion Reading Group for working through the manuscript with me.

Finally, much love to my wife, Ema Sani, for our many conversations on this topic. A question that has plagued our thoughts for quite some time is, "Why are we living in a world like this?" The partial answer that I give to this question in this book is in large part inspired by our conversations and co-authored work. Hopefully one day I will be able to give a more robust answer to that question, but when it comes to the making of many books there is no end.

Preface

ONE OF THE MOST important questions in life concerns the nature and existence of God. If God exists, what is God like? This is a question that has captivated my attention for many years, and has led me down the path to exploring different conceptions of the divine nature. What I present in this book are my current thoughts on the nature of God. This represents where I am in my current journey to understand the God whom I love and worship. It is my attempt to offer a concise statement of my previous academic work, and explore some uncharted territory. Academic books are often too long, and too expensive, making them inaccessible to most of the world. I wanted to write something that would be readily available to everyone who is interested in knowing more about God. Hence, a little book about a big God.

My hope is to present a conception of God that is biblical, philosophically rigorous, and spiritually satisfying. My problem is that I am not fully satisfied with the conception of God that I present. However, I take this to be perfectly understandable and acceptable. Part of the Christian life is a daily renewal of our minds as we draw closer to God (Rom 12:2). Since I have yet to be fully conformed to the image of Christ, it only makes sense that I would find myself with less than satisfying knowledge of exactly what God is like.

There is a sense in which my current dissatisfaction with my understanding of who God is and what God is like is rather mundane. There is nothing terribly interesting in the fact that I do not have a full grasp of God. If I did have a perfect grasp of what God is like, that would be very interesting indeed, but I have no such comprehension. This lack of full comprehension is rather mundane because the same thing is true of all my relationships with loved ones. I do not fully comprehend who these people are either. I am in the process of coming to know them, and in the process of coming to know myself. Allow me to explain.

As we draw closer to others in love and empathy, we are constantly reforming our thoughts about who this person is that stands before us. Over time, we slowly gain a deeper understanding of what our relationship together is all about. Coming to know someone well takes time. Empathy takes practice. When we come to know someone well, we are in a perpetual state of testing our ideas about this other person, and trying to discern if our beliefs and emotions fit with who they actually are.[1] In the process, we are sometimes presented with big questions that can shake our world. Is this person really who I thought they were? What does it say about me that I love this person? Can I trust this person with the things that are most precious to me? When we ask such questions, we open ourselves up to being changed by this other person. This person might change your mind about who they are. This person might change your heart for the better or worse. The relationship that you are building together might call upon you to transform your life entirely. That can be scary at the worst of times. That can be exciting at the best of times. Yet it can also be slow and boring too. These common experiences are part of the journey of life.

Things are no different when it comes to our relationship with God. The struggle to make sense of who God is takes time and practice. It requires of us to continually test our beliefs to see if they really fit with who God is. It demands that we make ourselves vulnerable to questions that can be scary or exciting. Is God really who I thought he was? Can I trust God with the things that are most precious to me? What does it really say about me that I love this particular conception of God?

The prospect of wrestling with such questions can elicit all manner of emotions. At times, the struggle to find answers might be really boring. I know from personal experience that some books about God are just plain boring. I assume that all of you reading this have had times in your prayer life and worship that struck you as a tedious chore. However, there are other times when dealing with such questions can range from excitement, pain, and joy. Finding out that your beliefs about God might be wrong can bring existential dread. Yet coming to a better understanding of God on the other end of a dark night of the soul can bring peace. The struggle to know God well is often a mixed bag of experiences. Consider that when Jacob wrestled with God, he limped away from his encounter, yet he was blessed (Genesis 32:22–32). As you wrestle with such questions, I pray that you walk away unscathed but not unmoved by the majesty of God.

---

1. Betzler, "Relational Value of Empathy," 20–21.

WHERE DO WE BEGIN?

I ask us to start with what I take to be the standard Christian story. This Christian story is stripped of various bells and whistles that different theological systems will wish to affirm, but the story contains a core that all Christian theological systems ought to be able to agree upon. After devoting several years to the study of Christian theology, I sometimes find myself at a loss to find what the standard Christian story ought to be. Some theologians will insist that certain obscure medieval doctrines that most people have never heard of, and that have zero biblical basis, are somehow essential to the story. Others will claim that certain selective portions of the Christian tradition are essential to the story. I say *selective* because everyone disagrees with some aspect or other of what Christians before them have said and done. For example, some wish to affirm all seven of the ecumenical councils, while others stop after the first four. In practice, most Christian theologians only have a rudimentary understanding of the three ecumenical councils that produced the Nicene Creed and the Chalcedonian Formula. Others will argue that different aspects of the ecumenical creeds are not only unbiblical, but also unnecessary to the standard Christian story. Yet they might have a statement of faith that contains a peculiarly long discussion on the nature of baptism in contrast to a rather meagre statement about the nature of God. Basically, Christian theologians disagree on a great many of things. In full awareness of this fact, I shall hazard an attempt at telling the standard Christian story. It goes a little something like this.

> Standard Christian Story: There eternally exists a triune God. From all eternity, this God has existed alone. This God freely decided to create a universe for a particular purpose. Part of this purpose includes satisfying the desire to enter into everlasting friendship with human persons, who are immaterial souls with physical bodies. In order for the friendship to be genuine, God ensured that human persons have rationality and freedom. These human persons rebelled against God, but God had anticipated this, and already had a plan to ensure that His purposes for creation would come to fruition. Part of this plan involved establishing covenants with particular groups of humans, as well as sending prophets to teach the people the ways of the Lord. The most dramatic part of this plan involved one of the divine persons becoming incarnate in human flesh in order to establish solidarity with humanity, as well as redemption. The reality of death might seem to go against God's desire for everlasting friendship, but God has accounted for this by offering an afterlife that comes in two stages. The first stage is called the

intermediate state. This is where a soul goes after it undergoes bodily death. The soul resides in the intermediate state until the second stage of the afterlife occurs. The second stage is the general resurrection of the dead in which all human persons are given new bodies, judged by God, and given everlasting life. At that point, sin and death shall be no more for God has completely defeated evil.

Notice that the standard story refers to various Christian doctrines. It contains the basic claims about the doctrines of God, creation, providence, anthropology, soteriology, and eschatology. I have tried to keep the standard story as generic as possible in order to allow different theological systems to add whatever details, bells, and whistles they would like. Allow me to point out some examples of how one might add to the content of the story, depending on her own theological beliefs about these different doctrines.

With regards to the doctrines of God and creation, I have stated that the triune God exists from all eternity, and that God creates a universe for a purpose. This doctrine of the Trinity could be a social model, a Latin model, or even something else. In other writings, I have defended a social model of the Trinity.[2] In an effort to keep this book short, I am largely going to ignore the doctrine of the Trinity. With regards to God's eternality, this eternity could be timeless or temporal, depending on one's theological commitments. Traditionally, many have affirmed that God is timeless. The Bible, however, knows nothing of a timeless God. Hence, in this book, I shall be articulating a temporal understanding of God's eternal existence. Notice that the standard Christian story does not specify what God's ultimate purpose is for creating the universe. It merely stated that part of the plan involves entering into everlasting friendship with creatures. God's ultimate plan might be for his own glory, or to increase value, or something else. Again, one can add to the story according to her own theological proclivities. I will have more to say on that in due course.

Another key component of the standard Christian story involves God's plan for ensuring that the created universe satisfies God's purposes. This refers to the doctrine of providence. As I will discuss later, there are different theories of providence on offer. I have tried to leave the standard Christian story generic enough so that different models of providence can be added on to it. Some views offer a very meticulous level of providence where God preordains every detail of history, whereas others offer a more general providence where God sets basic goals for creation and guides history accordingly.

2. See e.g., Mullins, "Divine Temporality, the Trinity, and the Charge of Arianism."

A further key factor of the story that can be extended is the final judgment or eschatology. I have merely stated that there is a final judgment and everlasting life. I said nothing about the quality of this everlasting life. If one believes in a doctrine of hell on which the damned suffer eternal conscious torment, one can say that the quality of this everlasting life will not be pleasant for certain individuals. If one affirms universal salvation, one will say that the quality of this everlasting life is going to be pretty great for everyone involved. Again, additions to the standard story can be made according to one's theological system of beliefs.

One will notice that the story has certain commitments that might not seem standard. For example, I state that God is alone from all eternity, and that humans are souls with bodies. One might complain that I have snuck in some rather thick theological claims that don't belong in the standard theological story. I disagree. These are standard claims. The majority of Christian theologians have affirmed a doctrine of creation out of nothing, which says that God existed alone prior to the existence of the universe.[3] To be sure, there are theologians who argue against this doctrine, and I have explored those issues elsewhere. What is important to point out is that these theologians openly acknowledge that they are arguing against fairly standard Christian claims when they reject the doctrine of creation *ex nihilo*.[4] The same goes for theologians who deny that human persons are souls with bodies, and who deny the interim state. These theologians openly acknowledge that they are arguing against fairly standard Christian claims.[5] In which case, they are not extending the standard story, but rather are amending the standard Christian story. In labeling these as amendments, I am not saying that these theological beliefs are mistaken. In fact, I am not making any judgment against such theological amendments in this book.

Part of the aim of this book is to consider different ways of extending and unpacking the standard Christian story as it relates to the nature of the eternal God. What is God like? What does God do? Those are going to be two important questions that will guide this study. But there are other important questions to ask that will help one answer those questions. Answering these questions has the larger goal of helping you know God well.

---

3. See Broadie, "Scotistic Metaphysics and Creation Ex Nihilo," 53. Fergusson, *Creation*, 40.

4. Cf. Oord, *Theologies of Creation: Creatio Ex Nihilo and Its New Rivals*.

5. See, e.g., Turner, *On the Resurrection of the Dead*.

KNOWING GOD WELL—WHAT QUESTIONS TO ASK?

I assume that you are reading this book because you want to know God well. Great! I also want to know God well. There are several important questions that need to be asked in order to come to a better understanding of God, and a deeper relationship with God. In this section, I will introduce you to some important questions to ask. These are questions that will be discussed in more detail as the book unfolds. What I offer here is just a taste of the things to come.

Here is one important question to ask. How do you know a person well? You know someone well if you learn their character traits and emotional profile. You learn what makes that person tick. You learn what they believe, and how to see the world through their own eyes. You come to understand what this person cares about, and what she is concerned with. When you care about something, you deem that object to be worthy of your attention and worthy of your action. If you don't care about something, you don't pay attention to it, and you don't think it is worth acting on. So learning what a person cares about will tell you a great deal about that person. This is because you come to see this person as a rational agent. You learn her reasons for why she thinks, feels, and acts in the ways that she does.

This brings me to the first important lesson for engaging in a study like the one contained in this book. If you want to know God well, you need to know what God is like, what God cares about, and the reasons or purposes for why God thinks, feels, and acts in the ways that he does.

Now as Christians, we don't just want to know God well. We want to have a close, personal relationship with God. Knowing someone well does not necessarily mean that you are in a close relationship with that person. To see this point, consider an FBI agent who is tracking a criminal suspect. The FBI agent could certainly say that she knows her criminal suspect well, but that definitely does not mean that she is going to be in a close, personal relationship with the criminal. If anything, these two people are *not* going to be described as having a close relationship. So I have to ask another important question. How do you have a close relationship with another person?

Close relationships take time, of course. Over time you come to know this other person well in the ways that I have previously described. As you come to know what this other person cares about, you start to share in some of those concerns. You figure out what goals or projects this other person has, and you find ways to support their goals as best as you can. We have many examples of this in our daily lives. Parents will often try to help their children figure out what the child wants to do with her life, and help their child figure out how to achieve those hopes and dreams. Friends will often share interests, and find ways to support each other's projects. These are ways that we develop close, personal relationships. We care about each other, and come to share in each other's cares and concerns, and we share in each other's projects.

When it comes to God, things are no different. If you want a close relationship with God, you need to share in God's cares and concerns, and support God's projects and goals. You need to figure out how you can best support God's projects and goals.

Of course, you are not going to get very far if you do not know what God's goal is or what God cares about. So we come to another set of questions. What does God care about? What are God's goals? Why did God create the universe? These are deep philosophical questions, but don't worry. Just because they are deep questions does not mean that they are scary. Sometimes these questions are scary. But sometimes the deep questions can be fun.

Here is a fun question that I will be exploring later in this book. What was God doing before he created the universe? In the fifth century, St. Augustine asked this question, and said that God was creating hell for people who ask those kinds of questions. This was a common joke in Augustine's day. He does not ask us to take this joke seriously. All jokes aside, I prefer the apostle Paul's answer to this question. What was God doing before he created the universe? There is a very real sense in which God was plotting to take over the world!

To see this, look at Ephesians 1:3–14:

> Blessed be the God and Father of our Lord Jesus Christ, who has blessed us in Christ with every spiritual blessing in the heavenly places, even as he chose us in him before the foundation of the world, that we should be holy and blameless before him. In love he predestined us for adoption to himself as sons through Jesus Christ, according to the purpose of his will, to the praise of his glorious grace, with which he has blessed us in the Beloved. In him we have redemption through his blood, the forgiveness of our trespasses, according to the riches of his grace, which he lavished upon us, in all wisdom and insight making known to us the mystery of his will, according to his purpose, which he set forth in Christ as a plan for the fullness of time, to unite all things in him, things in heaven and things on earth. In him we have obtained an inheritance, having been predestined according to the purpose of him who works all things according to the counsel of his will, so that we who were the first to hope in Christ might be to the praise of his glory. In him you also, when

you heard the word of truth, the gospel of your salvation, and believed in him, were sealed with the promised Holy Spirit, who is the guarantee of our inheritance until we acquire possession of it, to the praise of his glory.

I want you to notice several things about this passage. We get answers to some of our questions. First, we have a clear answer to our question, "what was God doing before he created the universe?" God was devising a plan to make us his children. Second, why did God create the universe? What was God's goal? I don't know all of the reasons for why God created the universe, but one reason is so that humans would exist and be his children. That is one of the goals or purposes for creating. God has a goal or a destiny for us in mind when he created the universe. Third, what does God care about? God cares about uniting us to himself. And he wants you to know that. Notice that Paul tells us that Christ has made known to us the mystery of God's will. God has a purpose. God has a project that he wants to accomplish. And God wants us to know what that project is.

I want to take a deeper look at this. There is something very important about the fact that God has made known his plan. This is an important theme in Paul's thinking, and in the Bible as a whole. In John 17, Jesus talks about the glory and love that he had with the Father before the foundation of the world. What was God doing before he created the universe? Jesus says that there was mutual love and glory among the divine persons of the Trinity. In John 17 Jesus tells us that he was sent so that all of us could have that same love, glory, and joy as well! Much like Paul, Jesus makes a big deal about how he has made the Father's plan known to us. What's going on here? Why is it such a big deal that God has made his plan known to us?

In John 15:1–17, we get an answer to this question. Here is what Jesus says:

> I am the true vine, and my Father is the vinedresser. Every branch in me that does not bear fruit he takes away, and every branch that does bear fruit he prunes, that it may bear more fruit. Already you are clean because of the word that I have spoken to you. Abide in me, and I in you. As the branch cannot bear fruit by itself, unless it abides in the vine, neither can you, unless you abide in me. I am the vine; you are the branches. Whoever abides in me and I in him, he it is that bears much fruit, for apart from me you can do nothing. If anyone does not abide in me he is thrown away like a branch and withers; and the branches are gathered, thrown into the fire, and burned. If you abide in me, and my words abide in you, ask whatever you wish, and it will be done for you. By this my Father is glorified, that you bear much

fruit and so prove to be my disciples. As the Father has loved me, so have I loved you. Abide in my love. If you keep my commandments, you will abide in my love, just as I have kept my Father's commandments and abide in his love. These things I have spoken to you, that my joy may be in you, and that your joy may be full. This is my commandment, that you love one another as I have loved you. Greater love has no one than this, that someone lay down his life for his friends. You are my friends if you do what I command you. No longer do I call you servants, for the servant does not know what his master is doing; but I have called you friends, for all that I have heard from my Father I have made known to you. You did not choose me, but I chose you and appointed you that you should go and bear fruit and that your fruit should abide, so that whatever you ask the Father in my name, he may give it to you. These things I command you, so that you will love one another.

There are all sorts of things going on in this passage. Here is the first thing I want you to notice. Why is it such a big deal that Jesus makes the Father's plan known to us? That is the difference between being a servant and being a friend. A master does not tell his servants what his projects are, or the reasons why he is doing various things. He just commands, and the servant is expected to obey. In this case, the master and the servant are not going to have a close, personal relationship. God wants more from you than that. God does not want us to merely be servants who blindly do what he commands. No. God wants us to be his friends. That is why God has gone to great lengths to reveal himself to us. To let us know what his goals are, and what he cares about. God wants us to know him well, and to be in a close, personal relationship with him. Why did God create us? What is God's goal? God created us with the goal of offering us genuine friendship. God wants us to be his disciples, but that is not the end goal. The end goal is genuine friendship.

Here is another important question that I want to ask. How do we become the kind of people that God can call a friend? We have part of the answer already. God calls us to love himself, love others, and to bear fruit. Loving God and loving others seems somewhat straightforward, but what is this whole thing about bearing fruit? The answer is in Galatians 5:22–23. The fruits of the spirit are love, joy, peace, patience, kindness, goodness, faithfulness, gentleness, and self-control.

I don't know about you, but I expect certain things from my friends. The people that I let get close to me need to have a particular character. A character that I can trust. God is the same. God expects us to become the kind of people that he can trust. People who are good, faithful, gentle, kind, and self-controlled. People who patiently strive towards peace. Joyful people who love one another. God wants us to become those kinds of people so that he can call us friends. That is one of God's goals—to enter into friendship with humanity. If you want to know God well, and have a close relationship with God, you need to figure out how to support God in his project of befriending humanity through the love of Christ.

With all of that in mind, I want to ask one more question. Do you want to be friends with God? That is a question that I cannot answer for you in this book. That is a question that requires some soul searching. That is one of the deep questions that can sometimes be scary. But my friendly suggestion is that though the question may be scary, the answer can be far more glorious.

1

What Is God?

This is a little book about a big God. My hope is that it will help you draw closer to God. As I stated in the preface, you can come to know a person well if you come to know her character and emotional profile, and what she cares about. I also said that you can develop a close, personal relationship with someone if you come to share in her cares and concerns, and promote her projects and support her goals. When it comes to God, things are no different. If you want to know God well, you will need to have some grasp of God's character, what he cares about, and what his goals are. In this chapter, we begin our journey by reflecting on the character or nature of God. I will start by asking the question, "What is God?" Then I will explain what divine attributes are, and briefly explore some different methods for discerning God's attributes.

WHAT IS GOD?

The first question to ask is quite natural. What is God? In other writings, I have distinguished between the core concept of God and models of God.[1] The concept of God is that of a perfect being who is the single, ultimate foundation of reality. That is a rather thin concept. It does not really tell you much about what God is like. Sure, it is good to know that God is perfect, or the greatest possible being. It is also nice to know that God is the ultimate foundation of reality. But what does any of that mean? What kind of attributes or characteristics does a perfect being have? What does it take to be

---

1. See, e.g., Mullins, "Creator/Creature Distinction."

the ultimate foundation of reality? A model of God attempts to answer those questions. Later in this book, I will help you think through some different models of God. For now, it will be helpful to say more about what a model of God is.

A model of God is a thicker conception, or particular extension of the core concept of God. A model of God tells you what it means for God to be perfect, and what it means for God to be the single ultimate foundation of reality. For example, some will say that God is the foundation of reality by creating the universe out of nothing. Others will say that God is eternally creating such that he always exists with a universe of some sort. One model of God might say that God's perfection involves God possessing certain attributes like immutability, which means that God cannot change in any way. Another model of God might say that this makes no sense. God's perfection involves being capable of changing in certain respects such as forgiving repentant sinners. If God cannot change from *wrath* to *forgiveness* when sinners repent, then how can God be perfect? As you can already see, theologians and philosophers have disagreements on what it means to be the perfect foundation of reality. I am going to try to help you navigate these disagreements by giving you some conceptual tools to think more clearly about these issues. In this chapter, I am primarily interested in the claim that God is perfect, and how one goes about understanding what it means to be perfect. In other words, I am interested in the essential nature or attributes of God.

WHAT ARE DIVINE ATTRIBUTES?

Philosophers talk about things having properties, qualities, characteristics, or attributes. There are different theories going on behind the scenes, but what is important to know is that a property or attribute is a feature that a thing has like a descriptive quality, an ability, or something similar. If you want to know what a thing is like, you describe it in terms of the properties or attributes that it possesses. When I am considering which politician to vote for, I am looking for a candidate with certain properties like moral integrity, strong leadership skills, and . . . well, who am I kidding? I usually look for the least corrupt candidate with some halfway decent policies. When I am considering which being is worthy of my worship, I set the bar much higher. I am looking for a being that has the best set of attributes. The property of *being the least corrupt* just won't cut it. As John Calvin explains,

> But although our mind cannot conceive of God, without rendering some worship to him, it will not, however, be sufficient

simply to hold that he is the only being whom all ought to worship and adore, unless we are also persuaded that he is the fountain of all goodness, and that we must seek everything in him, and in none but him.[2]

Calvin is setting the bar quite high, but that is to be expected if we are talking about the perfect God. The set of attributes that describe what God is like should be pretty spectacular and unique. An attribute like *being the least corrupt* does not seem like something that God would possess, whereas *fountain of all goodness* seems more appropriate.

If you want to know what God is like, you will need to identify which attributes God has.[3] There are various debates over how to classify the divine attributes. A standard prolegomena in systematic theology is the classification of the divine attributes. There are different ways of conceptually dividing up the attributes of God. For example, some talk of God's incommunicable and communicable attributes. Others distinguish between God's natural and moral attributes. The way that I prefer is to speak of God's essential attributes or properties on the one hand, and God's relative, accidental, or contingent attributes or properties on the other. Allow me to unpack this a bit.

An essence is a description of what a being fundamentally is. An essence identifies a set of properties or attributes that make a being the kind of thing that it is. For example, the essence of a human person might be something like *a rational soul embodied in human flesh*. No being can be considered a human person without that essential property. Further, an

---

2. Calvin, *Institutes of the Christian Religion*, 1.II.1.

3. There is a surprisingly bizarre tradition within Christianity which denies that God has any attributes. This is called the doctrine of divine simplicity. I have written extensively on this in the past, and believe that its incoherence should not be allowed to plague Christianity anymore. See, e.g., Mullins, "Simply Impossible"; Mullins and Byrd, "Divine Simplicity and Modal Collapse." Proponents of divine simplicity often assert that if God has distinct attributes, then God has parts and can thus come apart. The fact that this argument has been debunked since the early middle ages does not deter contemporary proponents from asserting it as gospel truth. For a brief statement of how the debunking goes, see Martin, "Simplicity's Deficiency." Most proponents of simplicity claim that the majority view within Judaism, Christianity, and Islam is to affirm divine simplicity. This claim is not born out by history since the doctrine does not seem to have been a mainstay in Jewish thinkers prior to Maimonides. Cf. Yoram Hazony, "Is God 'Perfect Being'?," and Diamond, "Living God." Further, the majority of Kalam theologians in the Islamic tradition openly reject divine simplicity in favor of God having distinct attributes. Cf. Harvey, *Transcendent God, Rational World*, ch. 4. The notion that simplicity has been a historical consensus within Western philosophical theology borders on propaganda. Moreover, there is no need for divine simplicity. All that is needed is divine unity. See O'Connor, "Unity of the Divine Nature."

essence is the set of properties or attributes that a being possesses no matter what. If you are essentially a human person, then you cannot cease to be a human person. If you could, then *being a human person* would not be essential to you. Instead, it would be accidental to you.

When philosophers speak of "accidental" properties, they are using this term in a technical sense. It does not refer to a mistake, or an unfortunate or unintended event, like it does in common English. Accidental properties are features that a thing has, but need not have. For example, my hair is brown. When I was younger, I dyed my hair blond to impress a girl who suggested that I would look really good with lighter hair. Having blond hair is not essential to who or what I am. It is an accidental feature that can come and go. Other accidental properties of mine cannot come and go, but they are still features that I need not have. I was born in Indianapolis. This is an accidental property that I have and I cannot lose it. I didn't have to be born there, so this property is not essential to me. Yet I will forever be a Hoosier because I was born in Indianapolis. I also have the property of *being a sinner* because I have committed some sins. That is not essential to what I am because those sins are actions that I freely performed. I did not have to perform those actions. Thankfully, I have another accidental property as well. I also have the accidental property of *being forgiven by God*. God's forgiveness of my sins is not essential because it is something that God freely and graciously decided to bestow upon me.

When it comes to God, things are no different. God has an essence, and God has various accidental properties.[4] The essential attributes of God are attributes that God would possess even if he had not created the universe. They are attributes that God has no matter what, and they describe what God is most fundamentally. Typically, these are attributes like necessary existence, maximal power, perfect goodness, and perfect freedom. The relative or accidental attributes, however, are attributes that only obtain if God creates a universe, or a particular kind of universe.

Allow me to clarify this a bit further because confusion abounds here in theology. Essential attributes are, by definition, not the sort of thing that a being can gain or lose. It is impossible for God to lose an essential attribute. As I will discuss in the next chapter, there are certain essential attributes that God has like maximal power, omniscience, and love. Thus, God cannot cease to be perfect in power, love, knowledge, and so on. Arguments to the effect that God is at risk of losing an essential divine property are more often than not deeply mistaken because they fail to understand the distinction

---

4. Some theologians balk at the idea of God having accidental properties, but the Bible sees things very differently.

between essential and accidental properties. Essential attributes are distinct from accidental attributes like *creator* and *redeemer*. Those are accidental attributes that God has if and only if he freely exercises his power to create a universe and redeem fallen creatures. If God did not freely create the universe, God would not have the accidental property of *creator*, but God would have all of his essential attributes. The accidental or relative attributes arise out of the exercise of God's essential attributes. For instance, Christian theologians typically say that omnipotence is an essential attribute of God's, whereas *creator* is a relative attribute. God would be omnipotent even if he did not create anything, but God would certainly not be the creator if he refrained from creating anything at all. God is only the creator if he freely exercises his omnipotence and creates something.

What I am interested in this chapter are God's essential attributes. In later chapters, I will investigate God's relative or accidental attributes. So, the next question to ask is this: How does one go about discerning which attributes are essential to God?

THEOLOGICAL METHOD

As I have studied different conceptions of God across the world's religions, there is one thing that everyone seems to agree on—God is perfect. Whatever exactly God is like, God is perfect, or the absolute greatest of all possible beings. People disagree over what God's perfection entails about him, but hardly anyone would deny that God is perfect. If you ask someone if she thinks God is perfect and she says no, you may very well conclude that you have encountered her on a bad day. Even the most sceptical of atheist philosophers who have investigated the existence and nature of God will agree that if God exists, then God is perfect. They just think that God does not exist. When I investigate different models of God, it is common for people to argue that their conception of God best captures the notion of perfection. They assure me that their model of God is way more perfect than their rivals. Yet, one will naturally ask how to discern which attributes a perfect being must possess.

There are different methods for developing an adequate model of God. There is a philosophical method for thinking about God that starts with the assumption that God is perfect. It is called *Perfect Being Theology*. Perfect being theology is not the only source for our knowledge about God, of course. God has revealed himself in creation, through prophets, and through Christ. This has led some theologians to say that God has given us two important sources of knowledge about himself—the book of nature and the book of Scripture. We can look at the natural world and make some fallible inferences about the nature and existence of God. We can also look at the revelations of God that are recorded in Scripture in order to adjust our thinking about the divine nature. In the rest of this chapter, I will briefly discuss these different methods, and try to draw together these different themes.

PERFECT BEING THEOLOGY

> Our knowledge of the Word comes from applying, in a raised degree, our own attributes to the transcendent nature. —Gregory of Nyssa[5]

Perfect being theology is a philosophical method used in the East and the West for determining which properties God has essentially and necessarily.[6] Perfect being theology is only designed to inform a person of God's essential properties. It is not a method designed to inform a person about God's contingent or accidental properties, like being the *creator of the universe*. In order to establish God's contingent properties, one will have to consider arguments from natural and revealed theology.[7] My main interest in this section concerns how to discern the essential attributes of God.

Perfect being theology starts by defining God as perfect, or the greatest possible being. The method of perfect being theology offers an analysis of what it means to be the greatest possible being, and then provides a few simple steps for discerning which essential properties the greatest possible being has.[8] The first question for a perfect being theologian to ask is this: What does it mean for God to be the greatest possible being? In order to answer this question, I need to introduce three concepts: great-making properties, extensive superiority, and intensive superiority.

I shall begin with great-making properties. Yujin Nagasawa says that some property *p* is a great-making property if, all else being equal, it contributes to the intrinsic greatness of its possessor.[9] Often times, philosophers and theologians state this as any property that it is intrinsically better to have than not have. A great-making property is an intrinsic property that would improve the greatness of any being that has it, and it would not worsen the

---

5. Hardy, *Christology of the Later Fathers*, 272.
6. Perrett, *Introduction to Indian Philosophy*, 199.
7. Morris, *Our Idea of God*, 28–35.
8. Speaks, *Greatest Possible Being*, 8–18.
9. Nagasawa, *Maximal God*, 53–55.

greatness of any being that possesses it.[10] A common great-making property is *goodness*. I take it as obvious that *goodness* is a property that is better to have than not have. Imagine if I pointed to something that lacks goodness, and I said to you, "Look at that great thing over there! Sure, it is a genuinely awful thing that has no goodness within it. But wow, isn't it great!" Surely you would think that I had gone mad or I was being sarcastic. Knowing me, the safe bet is that I am being sarcastic.

Perfect being theologians emphasize that great-making properties cannot entail any liabilities or imperfections. In the medieval tradition, theologians sometimes distinguished between pure perfections and impure perfections to help clarify our intuitions about great-making properties. Pure perfections are great-making properties like *power* or *knowledge*. Impure perfections are properties that make some beings better, but come with liabilities like *healthy lungs*. Having healthy lungs is pretty great for humans, but having lungs comes with liabilities like the potential for suffocation. That liability is less than great, so the perfect being theologian excludes this from the list of essential properties possessed by God.

When it comes to discerning which properties God has essentially, the perfect being theologian will say that God has whatever properties are intrinsically better to have than not have. Part of the method of perfect being theology is to identify these great-making properties, and predicate them of God. A common list of great-making properties includes *existence, personhood, power, knowledge, goodness,* and *freedom*. However, there is more at play in the method of perfect being theology.

Merely identifying a list of potential great-making properties is not enough to establish that God is the greatest possible being. To be the greatest possible being is to have extensive superiority and intensive superiority to all other possible beings. I shall define each concept in turn.

Nagasawa says that a being x is extensively superior to some being y if and only if x has all of the same great-making properties as y, and x has some great-making properties that y does not have.[11] For example, imagine two beings named Apollo and Chronos. Apollo and Chronos both have great-making properties like *power* and *goodness*, but Apollo has an additional great-making property like *knowledge* that Chronos lacks. In this case, Apollo is extensively superior to Chronos because Apollo has more great-making properties than Chronos. In the case of God, perfect being theologians say that God has all of the possible great-making properties, and is thus extensively superior to all other possible beings. As perfect, there

---

10. Nagasawa, *Maximal God*, 65.
11. Nagasawa, *Maximal God*, 56.

is no genuine great-making property that God could lack. After all, a being really can't be considered the greatest if it lacks some great-making features.

Extensive superiority focuses on the possession of multiple great-making properties, whereas intensive superiority focuses on the intensity of the individual great-making properties. Nagasawa says that some being x is intensively superior to some being y if and only if x has some great-making property that y has, but to a greater degree of intensity than y.[12] For example, imagine that Apollo and Chronos both have the great-making properties of *power* and *knowledge*. Apollo is intensively superior if Apollo has more *power* and *knowledge* than Chronos. The intuition is that whoever knows more must be greater, and whoever has more power must be greater. Upon reflection, it makes sense to say that the greatest possible being is going to have the greatest degree of knowledge and power. Otherwise, the being really is not the greatest.

In the case of God, perfect being theologians claim that God has all of his degreed great-making properties to the maximal degree of intensity. When it comes to degreed properties like *power*, *knowledge*, and *goodness*, perfect being theologians say that God has these great-making properties to the maximal degree. God is not just powerful, but maximally powerful. God's power is intensively superior to all other possible beings because God has the maximal degree of power. The same goes for God's knowledge and goodness. God has maximal knowledge and maximal goodness.

Notice that I said "degreed properties." I say "degreed properties" because some great-making properties do not obviously come in degrees of intensity. For instance, properties like *existence* and *eternality* are traditionally taken to be great-making properties, but they do not obviously have degrees of intensity in which they can be possessed. To be eternal is to exist without beginning and without end. One cannot have a little bit more or less of existing without beginning or end. To be sure, there are some people who say that some things can have more existence than other things, but I think that is just a confused way of talking. Things either exist or they do not.[13] There are no things that have just a little bit more of existence than other things.[14] If Apollo and Chronos both exist, it is just confused to say that Apollo has a bit more existence than Chronos. Perhaps "a bit more existence" is a polite way of saying, "Apollo is fatter than Chronos," but perfect being theologians are not interested in polite figures of speech. They are

---

12. Nagasawa, *Maximal God*, 57.
13. Merricks, "Only Way to Be."
14. McCann, *Creation and the Sovereignty of God*, 27.

interested in discovering the basic features of reality that make something truly great.

When it comes to talking about God's existence, theologians typically say that God necessarily exists. This means that God must exist. God cannot fail to exist.[15] It is absolutely impossible for God to fail to exist. If God must exist, then God exists without beginning and without end. This is because no being that must exist could have a beginning. Nor could a being that must exist at some point cease to exist. So perfect being theologians say that God is a necessarily existent and eternal being with other great-making properties like maximal power, maximal goodness, and maximal knowledge. I'll have more to say about God's essential great-making attributes in chapter 2. In this chapter, I am merely trying to provide you with a framework for thinking about God.

NATURAL THEOLOGY AND CREATOR THEOLOGY

Our intuitions about perfection are one source of knowledge about God. To be sure, it is a fallible source of knowledge since our intuitions can be mistaken. Yet it is a source none the less. As I said before, there are other sources of knowledge. Earlier, I mentioned the book of nature and the book of Scripture. Reflection on the book of nature is sometimes called *natural theology* or *creator theology*.[16] Natural theology and creator theology are often conflated, but I believe that these are actually distinct methods. I will start with natural theology.

When one is engaged in natural theology, one is looking at various features of the world and making reasonable inferences about the nature and existence of God. Well, hopefully one will be making reasonable inferences. Sometimes our inferences go awry, and other times they seem to be sound.

The apostle Paul tells us that by reflecting upon the natural world, we can infer God's eternality and power (Rom 1:20). The idea is quite simple. It makes sense that whatever brought about this contingent universe must be some eternal being with a great amount of power. Across the world's religions, philosophers have taken this basic idea and developed an abundance of arguments for the existence and nature of God.[17] Many of the arguments seek to establish that there is a necessarily existent, eternal being with a vast amount of power, knowledge, and goodness. This being is responsible for

---

15. Rasmussen, "Could God Fail to Exist?" McIntosh, "Why Does God Exist?"
16. Morris, *Our Idea of God*, 32.
17. Smart, *Doctrine and Argument in Indian Philosophy*.

the existence and nature of the world that we see around us.[18] According to Thomas Aquinas, this being is what all men call God.

Just as with perfect being theology, there are limits to what natural theology attempts to establish. Perfect being theology attempts to establish what God's essential attributes are. It does not tell us what God's accidental properties are. According to John Duns Scotus, perfect being theology can tell you that God is omnipotent and free, but it cannot tell you what God will do with that power and freedom. Natural theology is no different. Most philosophers interested in natural theology claim that natural theology can tell you that there is a necessarily existent being with certain essential attributes, and certain accidental properties like *being the creator*. Most claim that natural theology cannot establish that God is triune, or that God became incarnate. In order to know something like that, one would need God to reveal that kind of information in a special way. Regardless of its limits, natural theology is an important source for our reflections on the divine nature.

What about creator theology? Natural theology tends to focus on arguments for the existence of God. Creator theology, in its purest form, is not attempting to offer an argument for the existence of God. Instead, it is trying to offer a clear method for developing a robust conception of God just like perfect being theology attempts to do. Perfect being theology takes its starting point with the perfection of God. According to Jonathan Kvanvig, creator theology starts with the creatorship or sourcehood of God. This method starts with the notion that "God is fundamentally the asymmetrical source of all else."[19] From this starting point, it attempts to derive various claims. For example, it seems like an easy inference from sourcehood to omnipotence because God will need to have maximal power in order to be the asymmetrical source of all else.[20] From there, it might not be too difficult to infer omniscience, personhood, and other common claims about the nature of God.[21] This is because maximal power entails the power or ability to know all that it is possible to know, and knowledge and power are common properties of persons. I will have more to say about this in the next chapter. For now, I will simply state that creator theology is an important source for our knowledge of God.

---

18. See, e.g., Clarke, *Demonstration of the Being and Attributes of God and Other Writings*.

19. Kvanvig, *Depicting Deity*, 9.

20. Kvanvig, *Depicting Deity*, 76.

21. Kvanvig, *Depicting Deity*, chs. 4 and 7.

REVEALED THEOLOGY

Christianity claims that God has revealed himself in special ways through prophets and ultimately through Jesus Christ (Heb 1:1–2). These revelations are recorded in the Bible, and serve as a testimony about God's dealings with particular groups of humans. A common claim among Christian theologians is that the biblical witness about God is meant to be the ultimate authority for our theological doctrines and practice. The extent to which theologians are consistent with this claim is debatable. Often times, in practice, Christians place a greater weight on the authority of their favorite dead theologian than on the Bible.[22]

The idea of biblical authority is that whatever we want to say about God, it will need to have some kind of basis in Scripture, and not conflict with any clear biblical teaching. For example, the Bible consistently and clearly teaches that God is rich in empathy and compassion. It would be rather odd to have a model of God that claims that God does not literally have any empathy, and then try to say that this is consistent with the Bible. Of course, many theologians have done exactly that, but I do not suggest following in their footsteps on this issue. Instead, I think it is deeply important that Christians affirm a Christlike God.[23] If the so-called "great tradition" disagrees with the biblical portrayal of God, so much the worse for the tradition. As Christians, we do not worship dead theologians, but instead place our trust in the living God of the Bible.

BRINGING IT ALL TOGETHER

I have identified common sources for knowledge about God: perfect being theology, natural theology, creator theology, and revealed theology. How exactly do these fit together? To be honest, I am not entirely sure. I don't think there is a step-by-step set of instructions for how all of this fits together. I can simply say that you need to think long and hard about these things. In my own personal life, I am constantly in a state of going back and forth between these different sources, trying to see if my conception of God fits with things I know to be true from each source. Does this mean that I am being tossed about by every passing wind? Of course not. We all do this kind of back-and-forth with anyone that we love. We communicate with our loved ones to see what they are thinking and doing, and we adjust our

---

22. For a defense of biblical authority over tradition, see Nemes, *Theological Authority in the Church*.

23. McConnell, *Christlike God*.

beliefs about them accordingly. We are always in the process of trying out our beliefs to see if they fit the world around us. When we spot an inconsistency in our beliefs, we experience cognitive dissonance, and try to remove the inconsistency. It is just how our minds work. How exactly we do all of this is a complicated matter, but it is something that we regularly do. When it comes to God, things are no different. Though I cannot give a step-by-step guide to how to do this, I can give some examples that I hope will help.

Consider your intuitions about what kind of properties a perfect being would have. Some people might be worried that they are just making stuff up about what should be considered a great-making property. Brian Leftow has expressed that worry, but he says that Scripture can help. In the Bible, God has revealed himself as being great in power, knowledge, and goodness. If you are worried that your perfect being intuitions are on shaky ground, you can turn to the Bible to see what it says about God's greatness. If God has revealed himself to be a particular way, then it might be safe to say that those are potential great-making properties worth reflecting on. According to Leftow, you can carry on with the rest of perfect being theology after starting with the great-making properties revealed in Scripture.[24]

Here is another example. You might find yourself with a model of God that you take to be consistent with perfect being theology and natural theology. Yet, you are uncertain if it really fits with the Bible. Well, if you take the Bible to be the ultimate authority for your theological thinking, you might need to revise your model of God. The idea is that whatever we want to say about God, it will need to have some kind of basis in Scripture, and not conflict with any clear biblical teaching. For example, the Bible clearly and consistently proclaims that God is good and loving, rich in mercy and compassion, slow to anger and quick to forgive. God is patient in ways that far outstrip our patience, and he desires that all be saved. God grieves when people turn their back on him, and God rejoices when sinners genuinely repent. Any model of God that conflicts with these clear biblical teachings ought to be rejected, but the history of Christian thought has not followed through with this.

The overwhelming traditional view is that God is in a state of pure, undisturbed happiness, and that God cannot be influenced by creatures in any way, shape, or form. Further, the so-called traditional view has overwhelmingly claimed that God does not literally have any mercy, empathy, compassion, or sadness. Nor can God be grieved by your sins, or delight in your repentance because that would involve God being influenced by you. Despite the fact that this traditional view completely contradicts the

24. Leftow, "Why Perfect Being Theology?"

clear and consistent biblical teachings about the character of God, the vast majority of Christian theologians throughout the years have affirmed this traditional view.[25]

How could they affirm such an anti-biblical view on the nature of God? Traditional theologians would say that God does not really have any empathy, but he presents himself as empathetic in order to draw us closer to himself. Apparently, we are too childish, too immature, to handle the true revelation that God has no empathy, so God must reveal himself to us in ways that we can understand. The claim is that God must condescend to us, must speak to us, in ways that are easier for us to grasp.

This should be surprising. Surely, if so many theologians over the past 1,800 years have been able to discern the true nature of God in spite of God's condescension, this would suggest that such a condescension was unnecessary in the first place. Moreover, when adults condescend to speak to children, we try to say things that are easy to understand, but we also try to say things that are accurate. We typically do not tell children the exact opposite of the way things are, unless we are engaged in dad jokes. And yet, this is precisely what these traditional theologians are saying that God has done. God has consistently presented himself to us in the Bible as being rich in empathy. Yet these theologians are saying that God literally does not have any empathy. That is not condescension. That is a ruse! To be sure, Scripture does engage in many figures of speech, but figurative language always points to a literal reality. A figure of speech is rather poor if it points in the exact opposite direction of the literal reality it intends to convey.[26]

Consider Jeremiah 9:1. Here, God says that he wishes his head were a spring of water so that he could cry all the tears that he needs to in order to express how deep is his lament. That is a dramatic metaphor that clearly points to a particular literal reality—God is sad. Yet the traditional theologian tells us that this metaphor is really an act of divine condescension in which God really means to convey that he is in a state of pure, undisturbed bliss. I think the traditional theologian could not be more wrong. If God is actually in a state of pure, undisturbed bliss, this metaphor is not apt at all. In fact, I should think that God is a bit of dunce if he used a grief metaphor thinking that this would help us understand that he is actually extremely happy. Perhaps we should not say things that make God a bit of a dunce. That goes against the idea of God having perfect wisdom. So in reflecting upon what God has revealed, we have brought in our perfect being theology

---

25. For more on this, see Mullins, *God and Emotion*.

26. For more on figures of speech in Scripture, and the kind of God they are meant to portray, see Fretheim, *What Kind of God?*

to test for consistency. We know that an omniscient being cannot be a dunce, so an omniscient being cannot say or do things that would make him one.

Of course, matters actually seem much worse. There are certain kinds of people who regularly reveal themselves as being rich in empathy when in fact they have very little. These are called psychopaths. If God regularly reveals himself as being rich in empathy and compassion, but literally has none, it would be easy to infer that God is the ultimate psychopath. That would go against the idea that God is maximally good. Perhaps the lesson to learn from all of this is that one should not say things that entail that God is a psychopath.[27] Instead, we should do our best to think the greatest things about the perfect God.

---

27. For more on divine accommodation, impassibility, and psychopathology, see Mullins, "Closeness with God."

2

The Essential Attributes of God

IN THE PREVIOUS CHAPTER, I asked you to start your journey into investigating the essential character of God. In this chapter, I give an overview of God's essential attributes. In later chapters, I will take a closer look at some of these attributes, but it is best to start with a grand picture before focusing in on the details. I will introduce some different concepts related to God's eternal nature.

THE UNCONTESTED DIVINE NATURE

As I said before, God is the greatest possible being. Part of that claim means that God essentially and necessarily has all of the possible great-making properties. Further, God has all of the degreed great-making properties to the maximal degree of intensity. There is a particular set of uncontested great-making properties that most theologians and philosophers agree upon. In this section, I shall identify and define these great-making properties before turning to more controversial great-making properties.

The first uncontested great-making property is that God is a *personal* being.[1] I say *personal* instead of *a person* because Christianity affirms that God is a tri-personal being. Though it is very common for Christian theologians throughout history to simplify the conversation by speaking of God as a person. I shall follow this common practice for now. Following the lead of the sixth-century theologian Boethius, I say that a person is a thing with

---

1. This is prevalent in Eastern religious conceptions of God as well. See Bartley, *Theology of Ramanuja*, 70. Perrett, *Introduction to Indian Philosophy*, 200–216.

a rational nature. Boethius used this concept of person to speak of God and humans, and the doctrines of the Trinity and incarnation.[2] What is a rational nature? To further clarify, one might say that a person is an immaterial mental substance that has certain mental properties essentially.[3] A person is a thing with the essential capacity for thought, self-awareness, and intentional action. Sometimes a person is described as a center of consciousness with the capacity for thought, feeling, and intentional action.

There has been a fabricated controversy in recent years with *some* contemporary philosophers denying that God is a person, even going so far as to say that this is the traditional Christian view of God. The suggestion is that the classical view just is a denial that God is a person.[4] However, this claim is implausible for several reasons. First, the classical Christian tradition has been quite explicit that God is a person or three persons, and that personhood is a perfection that one must predicate of God.[5] I've already cited Boethius, so I shall consider other historical examples. According to Augustine, "It is not one thing for God to be and another to be a person, but entirely the same thing."[6] Peter Lombard repeats this by saying, "For God it is the same to be a person as to be, just as it is the same for him to be as to be God."[7] Second, the classical Christian tradition says that God has knowledge, power, goodness, and freedom. I find it difficult to discern how God can have these great-making properties without being a person.[8] Hence, I take it as historically false and conceptually confused that the classical Christian tradition denies that God is a person.

This fabricated controversy has been the source of some rather unfortunate Christian debates in recent years over the doctrine of God. This has led to all manner of conceptual confusion and mudslinging. I suggest that we never speak of this mistake again.

Another uncontested great-making property is that God is a necessarily existent person. What does it mean to say that God is a necessarily existent person? The notion of necessary existence typically comes with a cluster of attributes that are often conflated with it like aseity and self-sufficiency. These are distinct attributes, though these distinctions are not always recognized. Necessary existence is when a being must exist, and cannot fail

2. Boethius, *Trinity Is One God Not Three Gods*.
3. Swinburne, *Coherence of Theism*, 105.
4. See, e.g., Davies, *Reality of God and the Problem of Evil*, 61.
5. Marschler, "Substantiality and Personality in the Scholastic Doctrine of God," 85.
6. Saint Augustine, *Trinity*, 7.6.11.
7. Lombard, *Sentences Book 1*, XXV.1.2.
8. Wiertz, "Classical Theism," 45.

to exist. It might be the case that things other than God necessarily exist, like numbers, the laws of logic, and propositions. These might exist independently of God, or they might be necessarily dependent upon God.[9] Thus, necessary existence does not imply independent existence. Aseity is an attribute that describes God's independent existence, whereas self-sufficiency describes God's independent perfect essence. These attributes can be stated as follows:

> Necessary Existence: A being necessarily exists if and only if it cannot fail to exist.
>
> Aseity: A being exists *a se* if and only if its existence is in no way dependent upon, nor derived from, anything external to itself.
>
> Divine Self-sufficiency: A being is divinely self-sufficient if and only if that being's perfect essential nature is not dependent upon, nor derived from, anything external to itself.

Aseity is often assumed within perfect being theology. The intuition here is that a perfect being cannot be the greatest possible being if its existence is dependent upon something external to itself. The same goes for God's self-sufficiency. Much like aseity, self-sufficiency is often assumed within perfect being theology. The intuition here is that a perfect being cannot be the greatest possible being if its essential properties are derived from some other thing. One cannot be the greatest if one is derived from something else.

Aseity and self-sufficiency are often conflated with a thesis called *divine foundationalism*, but these are distinct claims about God. Divine foundationalism is the thesis that God is the first cause and fundamental ground—the diachronic and synchronic source—of all things that are distinct from God.[10] As already noted, this is one of the conditions for the concept of God. I shall have more to say about this later in the chapter on divine action and creation.

The next property to consider is maximal power or omnipotence. Omnipotence is the most power-granting set of abilities that is logically possible.[11] As T. J. Mawson explains, the maximal power-granting set does not simply contain all abilities. This is because not all things that we speak of in English as *abilities* are powers. Some abilities are liabilities.[12] For example,

---

9. Cf. Bohn, *God and Abstract Objects*.
10. Bohn, *God and Abstract Objects*, 2. Cf. Leftow, *God and Necessity*, 20.
11. Mawson, *Divine Attributes*, 41.
12. Mawson, *Divine Attributes*, 42.

the ability to perform irrational actions is a liability.[13] Thus, this ability will not be included in the maximal power-granting set of abilities because it is a weakness and not a power. One might also consider the ability to have false beliefs to be a liability, thus excluding this from the maximal power-granting set of abilities. This entails that having maximal cognitive excellency is an essential divine property.[14]

Maximal cognitive excellency involves all of the powers associated with beliefs, rationality, and emotions. I'll start with beliefs and knowledge. In part, this power is the ability to know all that is possible to know. I take this power to be more fundamental than God's possession of omniscience. This is because knowing something presupposes the power or ability to know something. Further, merely knowing something is not a perfection since it also matters *how* one knows things.[15] As maximally excellent in his cognitive abilities, God will acquire his beliefs in the best possible way, and his beliefs will accurately track reality. If God exists all alone, then God will know that he exists all alone. If God creates a universe, then God will know that he exists with a universe. He will not be mistaken about this fact. His beliefs are infallible. Any being that could be mistaken in their beliefs will not have maximal cognitive excellence. Further, God will not just find himself with true beliefs. God does not just happen to get lucky that his belief corresponds to reality. A being who just gets lucky is less than great, whereas a cognitively excellent being forms its beliefs in the right way.

Understanding God as having maximal cognitive excellence helps one avoid standard problems for omniscience. To see how this sort of dialectic might go, consider how Mawson defines omniscience. He says that for all true propositions, God knows that they are true, and for all false propositions, God knows that they are false.[16] This definition is fairly standard, but it runs into various problems such as the problem of *de se* knowledge.[17] This is first-person knowledge that is unique to a particular individual. The problem is that these are true propositions that God cannot know, which is a strike against omniscience. When Isaiah says, "Woe is me for I am a sinner in the presence of a holy God," this is a proposition that God cannot believe because God is a numerically distinct person from Isaiah.[18] God cannot know <I am a sinner in the presence of a holy God> because the *I*

---

13. Mawson, "Omnipotence and Necessary Moral Perfection are Compatible," 217.
14. Taliaferro, *Consciousness and the Mind of God*, 284.
15. Taliaferro, *Consciousness and the Mind of God*, 286.
16. Mawson, *Divine Attributes*, 34.
17. Grim, "Problems with Omniscience," 176–78.
18. This is my paraphrase of Isa 6:1–7.

there specifically picks out Isaiah. If God held such a belief, this would be less than cognitively excellent. It would simply be a muddled confusion. I take it that the potential to fall into a muddled confusion is a liability, and thus not included in God's maximal cognitive excellency.

As cognitively excellent, God has the power to know everything that it is possible to know. One can say that for any proposition that it is possible to know, God knows *of* the truth-value of those propositions.[19] In the case of *de se* beliefs, it is impossible for God to know things like <I am Isaiah>, but God can know of the truth-value of this proposition as it pertains to Isaiah. God will know that this proposition is true when uttered by Isaiah, and that it is false when uttered by himself.

A being with maximal cognitive perfection is also a perfectly rational being. God is perfectly rational if and only if God always acts for an objectively good reason. As Richard Swinburne maintains, "God is guided by rational considerations alone."[20] As I shall explain in due course, there are different kinds of values that serve as reasons for actions. For example, moral values are a common source of reasons for action. Hence, God's perfect rationality entails that God is morally perfect. Before seeing that entailment, I wish to draw out the entailment for God's emotional life because emotions involve responses to values.

As I said before, maximal cognitive excellence covers beliefs, rationality, and emotions. For the purposes of this chapter, I shall define an emotion as a felt evaluation of a situation. An emotion is a mental state with two components: cognitive and affective.[21] An emotion has a cognitive component in that an emotion is always about something, or it mentally represents the world as being a certain way or as having a certain value. An emotion is affective in that there is something that it is like to have an emotion. Your evaluation of the situation feels a particular way. When you have an emotion like happiness or sadness, you are happy or sad because of something in the world. You are evaluating something in your situation as being a proper object of happiness or sadness, and your evaluation feels a particular way depending on the content of the emotion.[22]

Since an emotion is cognitive, and involves an evaluation, emotions can be rational or irrational depending on how well they track reality, and how well in line they are with one's pattern of commitments and considered

---

19. Swinburne, *Coherence of Theism*, 177.
20. Swinburne, *Christian God*, 128.
21. Cf. Soteriou, "Ontology of Emotion."
22. See Roberts, *Emotions in the Moral Life*, 114–15. Todd, "Emotion and Value," 706.

judgments. The claim is that emotions allow one to perceive the value of objects in the world. An emotional response to an object is partly constituted by the way the individual perceives the value of the object.[23] An object has value to an agent if she perceives it to be worthy of her attention, and worthy of her to act on behalf of the object.[24] If an emotional response fails to properly track the value of the object, the emotional response is not rational. If an emotional response properly tracks the value of the object, the emotional response is rational.[25] Given God's maximal cognitive excellency, God's emotions will always properly track the values in reality.

The traditional Christian view is that God is always in a state of pure, undisturbed happiness that is entirely grounded in himself. For anyone who has read the Bible, this view ought to be considered as absurd since the Bible clearly describes God as experiencing a range of emotions such as sadness and anger as he interacts with a sinful world[26] (e.g., Exod 4:14; Judg 2:12; Isa 15–16; Jer 9:10 and 48:32). It should strike one as irrational and immoral for God to be in a state of pure bliss while his creatures suffer in misery. That hardly looks like a righteous being who experiences indignation toward sin every day (Prov 7:11). Further, the Bible does not say that God's happiness is entirely grounded in himself. The Bible constantly describes God has taking delight in his creatures (Isa 62:4–5). Genesis 1 contains a repeated refrain that God found delight in his creation because he saw that it is very good. This range of emotions is what one should expect from a God who is appropriately responsive to values.

At this point, it is worth mentioning that emotions are different from moods. Emotions are evaluations of particular objects and situations. Moods are rather different. Moods are often said to be about everything and nothing.[27] When you are in a bad mood, you see everything as absolutely terrible. When you are in a good mood, you tend to see everything as sunshine and rainbows. Because of this, philosophers typically say that moods are either arational or irrational.[28] Since God is perfectly rational, God does not have moods. This ought to bring a sigh of relief. No one will be arriving in heaven, and have to worry if she has caught God on a bad day. There will

---

23. Todd, "Emotion and Value," 706.

24. See Helm, "Emotions and Practical Reason," 195.

25. Todd, "Emotion and Value," 704.

26. For a thoughtful exposition of divine emotions in the Bible, see Lamb, *Emotions of God*.

27. For a different take on moods, see Tappolet, "Metaphysics of Moods."

28. Deonna and Fabrice, *Emotions*, 105.

THE ESSENTIAL ATTRIBUTES OF GOD   21

not be any angel on judgment day pulling you aside and saying, "Hey, God is in a really bad mood today. I would watch what you say."

As I understand things, God's maximal cognitive excellency entails that whatever emotions God has they must be consistent with perfect rationality, which in turn entails that God's emotions must be consistent with moral perfection.[29] Perfect rationality entails moral perfection because moral considerations are reasons for acting.

According to Mark C. Murphy, God is maximally good if and only if God is appropriately responsive to morally relevant values.[30] In this way, a morally good agent is rational because it is rational to be responsive to moral values. In articulating God's perfect moral goodness, Murphy explains that

> the sort of appropriateness of the response to value is *rational* appropriateness, simply acting in response to these values in a way that those values give reason to respond to them. To respond appropriately to morally relevant value is to do what there is good reason to do as a response to those values.[31]

Mawson agrees with the gist of this definition, but says that maximal goodness involves three objective moral dimensions: deontological, consequentialist, and virtue.[32] In agreement with Murphy, Mawson says a perfectly good person always does what he has most objective reason to do. As maximal in cognitive power, God will always know what he has most objective reason to do. As omnipotent, God will be free to perform the action that he has most objective reason to do.[33] Further, a perfectly good God is one whose intentions are always good, and who never fails to satisfy his obligations. A perfectly good God's actions will give rise to the best possible consequences. In performing these good actions, God will instantiate virtuous character traits such as generosity, wisdom, compassion, and so forth.[34]

Notice that Mawson claims that God's power entails freedom. This is because free will is an ability or power to perform intentional actions for a reason. Swinburne concurs. Since God is perfectly rational, God is said to be perfectly free in that no non-rational causes act in or on God to influence him to perform his intentional actions.[35] To see this entailment, one must

---

29. Cf. Mullins, "Why Can't the Impossible God Suffer?" Ekstrom, "Practical Life of God," 114.

30. Murphy, *God's Own Ethics*, 25.

31. Murphy, *God's Own Ethics*, 25.

32. Mawson, *Divine Attributes*, 47. Cf. Wiertz, "Classical Theism," 44.

33. Mawson, *Divine Attributes*, 50.

34. Mawson, *Divine Attributes*, 47. Cf. Leftow, "Infinite Goodness."

35. Swinburne, *Coherence of Theism*, 142.

understand what freedom is. An agent is free in that (i) the agent is the source of her intentional actions, (ii) performs her intentional actions for a reason, and (iii) is in control of her actions in that she is able to perform or refrain from performing her intentional actions.[36] Allow me to unpack each of these conditions a bit further.

An intentional action is an action that one intends to perform in order to bring about some particular goal. Free actions are thus goal-oriented. The goal is often one of the reasons motivating a particular action because the agent sees the goal as something worth bringing about. Hence, free actions are actions performed for a reason. According to Kevin Timpe, if an agent lacks a reason at a particular time to perform an action, then the agent is incapable of performing a free action at that particular time.[37] The strength of one's reasons to perform any given action vary. In many cases, our actions are not performed for decisive reasons that compel us to perform them. Instead, we often act on various justifying reasons, or considerations that rationally justify us to act a particular way. These are weaker than decisive reasons that compel us to perform certain actions. Hence, one is often capable of performing or refraining from performing a particular action.

Given God's aseity, self-sufficiency, and power, God is the source of his actions. Thus, God satisfies condition (i). Given God's maximal cognitive excellency, God will have the power to know all of the relevant reasons for performing any given action. Thus, God will be able to satisfy condition (ii). When it comes to condition (iii), things become more complicated. As I understand it, if there is a best action to perform in a given situation, then God is rationally compelled to perform that action. A best action is one that best satisfies whatever goals or purposes God desires to accomplish. However, it seems plausible that in many situations God is not presented with a best action, and is thus capable of performing or refraining from any number of actions to satisfy his desired end. Thus, God is capable of satisfying condition (iii).

God's power does not merely entail that he is a being with free will. As omnipotent, God's freedom is maximally efficacious. A free action is efficacious if the action brings about the goal that the agent intended to bring about. A free action is not efficacious if the action fails to bring about the agent's intended goal.

To illustrate this point, consider the following: Imagine that God's will is not efficacious. Perhaps there is an indeterministic link between God's

---

36. Rea, *Metaphysics*, 152–54; Pruss, "Divine Creative Freedom," 213–14. Erickson, *Christian Theology*, 378.

37. Timpe, *Free Will in Philosophical Theology*, 23.

causal power and all of the effects that God intends to bring about. This may sound like an implausible claim, but some contemporary classical theists have posited this thesis in a desperate attempt to salvage the unbiblical doctrine of divine simplicity.[38] On this scenario, God can intend to bring about a particular state of affairs, and that state of affairs can fail to obtain. This is because merely willing that something obtain would not determine that this state of affairs comes to be realized. Imagine that God intends to create a universe in which a single electron spins in the void. Surely creating a single electron would be a simple task for an omnipotent being. Yet, if God's will is indeterministic in this way, God could very well fail to create an electron. When God intends to bring about the existence of the electron, God would not be certain what the end result would be. The same is true for any action that God might perform. For any divine action, God would not be certain what the result would be. This hardly sounds like an omnipotent being.

Traditionally, theologians have affirmed the infallibility of omnipotence. This is the thesis that if God intends to bring about some state of affairs S, then S must come about. There is no way for God's actions to fail to bring about his intended effect. That certainly sounds like an omnipotent being because maximal power entails the maximal efficacy of the will.

Yet there is the biblical theme of God's unfulfilled desires.[39] Various passages speak of God's desire to save everyone, and yet other passages seem to imply that not all humans are saved (2 Pet 3:0; John 3:16; Matt 22:14). How is the efficacy of God's will to be understood in light of these biblical passages? There might be certain states of affairs that God cannot guarantee the outcome of because of the kind of thing that God is attempting to bring about. Surely if God intends to create a universe with a single electron, he can guarantee the outcome. Yet perhaps God cannot guarantee certain outcomes when creating beings with their own freedom. In which case, God's intentions should be understood differently. If God wants to create beings with free will, then he can certainly do it. That is not the issue. The issue is if God can guarantee what choices free creatures will make. Theologians disagree on this point. Some say that God can guarantee which choices free humans will make, and others say that God cannot guarantee human free choices in advance. For the moment, consider the claim that God cannot guarantee what humans will freely chose to do. In this case, God's action is still efficacious. God intended to create beings with free will knowing full

---

38. For more on the biblical evidence, or lack thereof, for divine simplicity, see Peckham, *Doctrine of God*, 225–35. Cf. Diamond, "Living God." Hazony, "Is God 'Perfect Being'?"

39. Peckham, *Divine Attributes*, 5–6. Cf. Anderson, "Election, Grace, and Justice."

well that this means he cannot control them, and he got exactly that. This is a debate that I shall return to later in this book.

There is one final great-making property that is widely uncontested—divine eternality. A being is eternal if and only if it does not begin to exist and does not cease to exist.[40] God's necessary existence entails that God is an eternal being.[41] This is because a necessarily existent being cannot begin to exist, nor fail to exist. However, there is a complication because eternality has been understood in two different ways throughout Western history: timeless or temporal.[42]

To say that God is timeless is to say that God necessarily exists without beginning, without end, without succession, and without temporal location. To say that God is temporal is to say that God necessarily exists without beginning and without end. However, the divine temporalist will deny that God necessarily exists without succession and temporal location. The temporalist will say that God must undergo succession as God freely exercises his power. The free exercise of divine power entails a change from *not acting* to *acting*.[43] Hence, God must be temporal because God undergoes succession and change when God exercises his freedom. It would also seem that temporality follows from God's maximal cognitive excellency since God's beliefs and emotions must change in order to track the values in reality. For example, God's beliefs change from "I exist alone," to "I exist with the universe that I have created." God's emotions change from anger to happiness when a sinner repents, and so on. In this book, I will primarily be concerned with divine temporality since that is the only view that the Bible knows, and it seems to me to be the most rational and coherent view.[44]

WHAT ABOUT LOVE? A DEEPER LOOK AT GOD'S GOODNESS

In recent years, some have argued that divine love is not an essential divine attribute. The claim is that love is not a perfection. Love does not really add anything to our understanding of what it means to be perfectly good, so we can dispense with talking about God being perfectly loving.[45] This

---

40. Wiertz, "Classical Theism," 44.

41. Clarke, *Demonstration of the Being and Attributes of God and Other Writings*, section V.

42. Mawson, *Divine Attributes*, 3. Cf. Melamed, introduction to *Eternity*.

43. Kittle, "Against Synchronic Free Will."

44. Mullins, *End of the Timeless God*.

45. Murphy, *God's Own Ethics*, 29–43.

is wrapped up in the notion that God's goodness is not moral goodness. Perhaps moral goodness is not even a divine perfection at all.[46] Yet such accounts of divine goodness devoid of moral perfection and love have left various philosophers feeling cold. This is because this account of divine goodness is consistent with God having no obligations toward the well-being of his creatures. Laura W. Ekstrom says that this is wildly implausible because this account of God's goodness is consistent with God enjoying the beauty of a tsunami as it destroys countless lives.[47] Such a view seems perverse.[48] Any notion of God that does not include moral goodness as an essential attribute is not in fact a notion of God at all. It is a monstrosity not worthy of worship.[49]

I want to say something even stronger. It is not enough to affirm that God is essentially morally perfect. The account of God's moral perfection that I have offered above is incomplete, almost heartless. Something is missing from our analysis of God's goodness if we do not see God's goodness as involving love.[50] Given this, it must be asked what is love.

In my book *God and Emotion*, I considered the classical claim that God's love is unresponsive to the values of creatures and found it wanting.[51] My focus was on what is classically called the two desires of love. Classically, love is said to involve a desire for the good of the beloved, and a desire for union with the beloved. I argued that these two desires cannot be satisfied unless God has empathy. I will return to divine empathy in the next section. For now, I want to focus on love, and point out something that I did not address in *God and Emotion*.

As I have said already, God is perfectly good if God is appropriately responsive to values. This is systematically connected to God's perfect rationality. As perfectly rational, God will always be appropriately responsive to reasons, and moral values are one source of reasons. The question, then, is what values are worthy of God to respond to. What does God care about?

The classical theist says that God is the highest good, and nothing of lesser value could move or influence God in any way. In other words, God's own value is the only value worthy of God to respond to. The value of creatures is not worthy of God's response. So God acts rationally and morally if and only if he is appropriately responsive to himself. Hence, why the

46. Murphy, "Is an Absolutely Perfect Being Morally Perfect?," 95.
47. Ekstrom, "Practical Life of God," 119.
48. Craig, "Molinist Response," 147.
49. Calvin, *Institutes of the Christian Religion*, Book 1.II.1.
50. Wessling, *Love Divine*, 176.
51. Mullins, *God and Emotion*, ch. 4.

classical theist says that God's love is unresponsive to the value of creatures, and God's love is really only self-love.

This classical understanding of God leaves the Christian with a curious notion of God's goodness, love, and rationality. To start, God has no reason to create anything at all since the values of possible creatures are not appropriate objects of divine response.[52] Thus leaving us with an arbitrary creation. Further, God has no reason to love his creatures, nor any reason to engage in self-sacrificial acts on behalf of his creatures. Any self-sacrificial acts on God's part would seem to be utterly arbitrary.[53] Why die for creatures that you do not deem to be worthy of responding to? On a divine whim? That hardly seems like a fitting reason for the cross. Yet the problem is deeper than this.

The God of classical theism can only act on behalf of his own self-interest since his own goodness is the only value that it is appropriate to respond to. Self-sacrificial acts are, by definition, not in one's own self-interest. Thus, the God of classical theism cannot perform self-sacrificial acts.[54] That hardly looks anything like the Christlike God who dies for the sake of his beloved children. As I see it, the God of classical theism cannot be considered loving nor morally perfect. It should come as no surprise, then, that a contemporary classical theist would argue that love and moral goodness are not really divine perfections![55] For this, and many other reasons, Christianity is simply incompatible with classical theism.[56]

There is another issue that I did not discuss in *God and Emotion* pertaining to God's love. The classical notion of the two desires is interesting, but it leaves unanswered a deeper question. Why does God love me? On the classical understanding, God cannot be said to desire my well-being because God cannot be responsive to my value nor the value of my well-being. Nothing outside of God is valuable enough to be worthy of his attention and worthy of his action. Nor would it make sense for God to desire union with me because my value is not an appropriate object of divine response. Any such desire would be utterly arbitrary.[57] That is hardly what one would expect from a perfectly rational being.

---

52. Mullins, "Problem of Arbitrary Creation for Impassibility."
53. Scrutton, *Thinking Through Feeling*, 135.
54. Wessling, *Love Divine*, 83–98.
55. See, e.g., Murphy, "Is an Absolutely Perfect Being Morally Perfect?"
56. Cf. Oord, *Pluriform Love*.
57. Wessling, *Love Divine*, 74.

There is a solution to this problem. To start, one should abandon classical theism in favor of a Christlike God.[58] Next, the solution to this problem is to give a deeper analysis of love that explains why God would desire the well-being of creatures, and desire union with creatures. Love fundamentally involves valuing things, and valuing things leads to desires toward those objects. To love something is to value that thing's existence and well-being, and to value union with it. When God loves a created person, God thinks that there is value in that person existing. God deems that this person is worth existing. God also deems that this person's well-being or flourishing is something that is worth promoting. A created person's highest good is a right relationship with God and others. As such, in promoting a person's flourishing, God deems that there is a great value in being in union with this person.[59]

Return to the desires of love. Why does God love you? Because God sees your intrinsic value and deems you to be worth creating and sustaining in existence. Why does God desire your well-being? Because God sees your intrinsic value and deems your flourishing to be a worthy goal for God to promote. Why does God desire union with you? Again, because God sees your intrinsic value and deems friendship with you a worthy thing to pursue.

I believe that more can be said about God's love. There is a distinction between emotions, character traits, and sentiments that will help us understand divine love. Emotions, character traits, and sentiments are grounded in one's cares and concerns. As I said before, one's emotions are about what one is concerned with, or deems to be worthy of attention and action. Sometimes certain cares and concerns become so ingrained in an individual that she develops a stable disposition toward the objects of her cares and concerns. These stable dispositions can become part of her character. For example, consider character traits like kindness or cruelty. A kind person is generally disposed to act toward others in a particular manner that is far different from how a cruel person is generally disposed to act. This is because a kind person deeply cares about values like *respect for other persons*. She cares so much about this value that she is generally disposed to act in accordance with this value in her daily life. This character trait can also explain why she feels different kinds of emotions in different situations. When a kind person sees someone suffering, she might feel sad, whereas a cruel person might feel delight. The difference in emotional evaluation is partly explained by the difference in character traits.

58. McConnell, *Christlike God*.
59. Wessling, *Love Divine*, 65.

Sentiments are similar to character traits. Character traits are focused on general values, whereas sentiments are focused on specific things. Julien Deonna and Fabrice Teroni say that love and hatred are paradigmatic cases of sentiments.[60] A sentiment is a stable disposition of valuing a particular thing, or caring deeply about a particular thing. A sentiment can ground an array of different emotions depending on the situation. To see this, consider your own life. Think about the people that you value so much that you can say you love them. When they are happy, you are happy for them. When tragedy befalls them, you are sad because you deeply care about them. When someone wrongs them, you might be ready to take serious action because how dare anyone hurt your loved ones!

When Christians say that God is a loving being, it sometimes sounds like a character trait, and other times it sounds like a sentiment. First John 4:7–21 seems to alternate between both of these predications. This passage says that God is love, which I take to be an essential character trait of God. Yet the passage also describes how this character trait is expressed in terms that sound more like a sentiment. This is because God's love is focused on us. God loves us so much that he sent his son to die for us. I'm uncertain exactly how to parse this, but my suggestion is something like this. God essentially has the character trait of *loving*, and God acquires sentiments toward his creatures after he decides which specific creatures to make.

DIVINE COMPASSION AND MAXIMAL EMPATHY

There is another essential character trait that God has—compassion. The Bible consistently describes God as a compassionate being. Psalm 103:13 says that God has compassion for those who fear him. Lamentations 3:22 says that God's compassion never fails (cf. Isa 49:15). What is remarkable is that the traditional Christian view is that God is not literally compassionate. Instead, God is only metaphorically compassionate.[61] Why? The traditional view is that God cannot suffer, nor can God be moved or influenced in any way by anything outside of himself. This is deeply contrary to what the Bible says about God. As John C. Peckham explains, "the biblical language of *compassion* explicitly depicts 'suffering along with,' akin to sympathy/ empathy, that is, [a] responsive feeling of emotion along with and for the object of compassion."[62] When the tradition says that God is only metaphorically compassionate, what they mean is that God does not suffer nor

---

60. Deonna and Teroni, *Emotions*, 108.
61. Anselm, *Proslogion*, viii. Davies, *Reality of God and the Problem of Evil*, 234.
62. Peckham, *Love of God*, 178.

empathize with you. God is not moved to think, feel, or act by anything outside of himself. Yet somehow, God still acts in ways that are considered compassionate.

Despite the long history of viewing God as metaphorically compassionate, I find this deeply implausible.[63] William Hasker says the denial of divine compassion "is not at all what most of us would expect of a being who is said to be perfectly loving! And it is also difficult to reconcile with the Scriptures, according to which 'As a father has compassion for his children, so the LORD has compassion for those who fear him' (Psalm 103: 13)."[64]

In my view, God is literally compassionate, but what exactly does that mean? According to Anastasia Scrutton, compassion is one kind of response on the basis of empathy.[65] Compassion is a beneficent action toward someone on the basis of having empathy with that person. You first empathize with that person, and come to understand what it is like for them to think and feel the way that they do. On the basis of this, you perform some action for that person's well-being and flourishing. Since compassion is one kind of response based on empathy, I need to say something about God's empathy.

I think that there is another power that is included in God's maximal cognitive excellency. This is the power to accurately empathize with others. The ability to empathize with others is the ability to understand how and why someone thinks and feels the way that they do. The knowledge gained from empathy provides unique reasons for action because the knowledge gained through empathy is a unique kind of knowledge.

Earlier I said that God does not just luckily find himself with the right beliefs. Perfect cognitive power entails forming beliefs in the right way that fully and accurately track reality. God does not just find himself with the belief that you are feeling sad or happy today. God fully grasps that you are sad or happy, and why you feel that way. How? Through empathy.

What is empathy? Empathy is coming to know what it is like for someone to feel a particular way. Hence, empathy is a state that one achieves. Much like emotions, empathy involves a cognitive and an affective component. Imagine that you are trying to achieve empathy with someone named Ben. There are three conditions that must be satisfied in order to achieve empathy with Ben. First, you need to know that Ben has some particular emotion. Second, you need to know what it feels like to have that particular emotion. Third, something about your interaction with Ben is the basis for

---

63. For a historical overview of the denial of literal mercy, empathy, and compassion, see Mozley, *Impassibility of God*.

64. Hasker, "Non-Classical Alternative to Anselm," 14.

65. See Scrutton, *Thinking Through Feeling*.

you coming to understand what it is like for Ben to feel that particular emotion. Let me unpack this a bit further.

Consider the first condition. Let's say that Ben is feeling happy because he has received a lovely birthday gift from his mother. If you think that Ben is feeling sad, you are not off to a great start with empathizing with him. You need to know that Ben is feeling happy. You also need to have some cognitive grasp on the reason for why Ben is feeling happy. The better you grasp the reason for why Ben is feeling happy, the more accurate your empathy is with Ben. If you were to say to Ben, "I understand your happiness over your new job," Ben will likely say, "You don't understand me at all." So it is important to understand which emotion Ben actually has, and the reason for why Ben has that emotion.

Next, consider the second condition of empathy. In order to empathize with someone, you need to know what it is like to have that emotion. If you can't really understand someone's situation, or what they are going through, then your ability to empathize with them is quite limited. Imagine that Ben is sad because he has lost his child. Parents who have never lost a child will often say, "I am sorry for your loss. I cannot imagine what you must be going through." Obviously these parents understand the emotion of sadness, so they can have a limited grasp on what Ben is feeling. Yet they are recognizing something important in stating that they cannot fully grasp Ben's situation. Our complex emotions come in many textures, and the grief of a lost child involves many such textures that are difficult to express to others who have not experienced them. This is why we often seek out support groups filled with people who have gone through similar experiences. We desire to be understood. There is a great value in being understood through empathy, and I will return to this theme in due course.[66]

Finally, consider the third condition for empathy. In order to achieve empathy with Ben, you need to come to understand what it is like for Ben to feel the way that he does. The third condition specifies that the way you come to understand this must be based on Ben in some way. If Ben has nothing to do with your knowledge, then it is difficult to say that you are in fact empathizing with Ben. There are many ways for others to influence your path toward empathy. Sometimes you can just look at a person and know what they are thinking and feeling. Two close friends can give each other knowing glances from across the room. Other times empathy is a bit more difficult to achieve. You might need to speak with Ben directly, or read his testimony, or hear about his thoughts from others. You might try to imagine Ben's situation, but your imagination will need to be checked

---

66. Morton, "Empathy and Imagination."

up against what Ben actually thinks and feels. This is important because empathy is not you adopting Ben's perspective on the world, nor is empathy you confusing your view on the world with Ben's. Empathy is you coming to know what it is like for Ben to think and feel as he does.

Let's bring God back into the conversation. How much empathy does God have? I think that God has the maximal degree of empathy possible with any given creaturely conscious state. Philosophers disagree over what that maximal degree is, and whether or not there are certain constraints on God's empathy. Linda Zagzebski has argued that God's empathy is an attribute called omnisubjectivity. This is the ability to have a perfect grasp of all creaturely conscious states.[67] As Zagzebski sees things, there are no constraints on empathy. On omnisubjectivity, God just automatically grasps all creaturely conscious states. There are theologians who will disagree with this notion. Peckham claims that God "does not essentially feel all the feelings of others indiscriminately."[68] The idea here is that there are certain moral and rational constraints on divine empathy such that God cannot empathize with all creaturely conscious states, though God can empathize to the maximal degree that is consistent with God's rationality and goodness.[69] Perhaps God cannot fully grasp what it is like for you to delight in an incredibly wicked sin. It might be that perfect goodness prevents God from fully grasping the delight in wickedness. I'm unsure. Personally, I go back and forth between these views on divine empathy. At the very least, I feel confident that part of God's cognitive excellency is the ability to empathize with others to the most accurate degree possible.

God's ability to empathize is important for various reasons. According to Zagzebski, God's ability to empathize is important for filling out the concept of omniscience since the experiential knowledge gained through empathy is a distinct kind of knowledge that has been neglected in many theological meditations. Zagzebski also thinks that God's empathy is important for filling out God's moral goodness. For Zagzebski, God's perfect empathy is a prerequisite for God being a perfect moral judge. If God does not fully understand what and why you are thinking, feeling, and acting a particular way, then he cannot properly judge you. Since God does know you from the inside out, he can be a perfect moral judge.[70]

There is another reason to stress the importance of divine empathy. With empathy comes intimacy. As I stated in the preface, it is through

---

67. Zagzebski, *Omnisubjectivity*.
68. Peckham, "Qualified Passibility," 101.
69. Mullins, "Problem of Arbitrary Creation for Impassibility," 64–69.
70. Zagzebski, "Omnisubjectivity," 448.

empathy that we draw closer to one another. Through empathy, two people can continually develop a better understanding of one another. Empathy plays such a crucial role in coming to know someone well, and in developing close, personal relationships. The fact that God has maximal empathy allows us to infer that a close, personal relationship with God is not only possible, but plausible. It also allows us to infer that our lives matter to God.

According to Francis McConnell, humans "want to feel that their suffering means something at the center of the universe. It means that they crave at least to be understood through the understanding which comes out of sympathetic sharing of distress."[71] Adam Morton points out something similar. He says that human persons desire to be treated empathetically, but that humans don't like it when the empathy is faked. We want the empathy to be genuine. "We resent empathy that is automatic and based on superficial aspects of our behaviour."[72] Imagine a situation in which you are crying, and someone superficially says, "Oh you poor thing." Morton says that you will likely be annoyed by this because the other person is not actually bothered by your situation. He also says that you will likely stop trying to explain your feelings to this other person because they are clearly not interested in, or not capable of, understanding your situation. In which case, the possibility for a close, personal relationship breaks down.

Morton writes,

> Life is full of situations in which you want someone to feel a congruent emotion, but want her to feel it for the appropriate reasons. We want accuracy. And inasmuch as empathy serves a central role in human life, we want it to be more or less accurate. Some of the reasons for this are clear. We don't bond with people who misunderstand us, because they are likely to misjudge our feelings and preferences on other occasions. And there are times when knowing the reasons for our emotions is needed for helpful action.[73]

Morton has in mind relationships between humans, but I think the same applies to our relationship with God. If God cannot empathize with humanity, it can easily lead one to wonder why she should bother caring about God. Why bother trying to explain your situation to a being that cannot possibly understand what it is like to be you?

Morton says that there are other reasons that we desire accurate empathy. He writes, "There is a kind of loneliness that comes when people cannot

71. McConnell, *Is God Limited?*, 290.
72. Morton, "Empathy and Imagination," 183.
73. Morton, "Empathy and Imagination," 183–84.

grasp why you feel what you do."[74] Knowing that no one else really understands your situation, what you are going through, leaves a person feeling isolated and alone in this vast universe. Humans need to be understood, and as such crave genuine empathy. Thankfully, we worship a God who can satisfy this need to the fullest!

---

74. Morton, "Empathy and Imagination," 184.

3

The Eternal God Without Creation

As I said in the previous chapter, to be eternal is to exist without beginning and without end. The standard Christian story says that God is eternal, but that creation is not. As John of Damascus explains, "It is not natural that that which is brought into existence out of nothing should be co-eternal with what is without beginning and everlasting."[1] The created universe began to exist, whereas the eternal God did not begin to exist. This entails that prior to creation, God was all alone. According to Samuel Lebens, creation ex nihilo can be understood as the affirmation that "the universe was created by God at some point in time (perhaps the *first* moment in time), before which there was nothing (except God)."[2]

God all alone has played an important role in Jewish, Christian, and Islamic thinking about God's nature, his free will, and his providential plan for the created universe. Today, many theologians get squeamish talking about God prior to creation. There are various reasons for this unease. Some think that we just don't know enough to really speculate about what God was like prior to creation. Others think that all knowledge of God begins with Jesus Christ, and there is something unseemly in thinking about God apart from Jesus Christ. As I see it, these worries are misguided. The Bible declares that God has made himself known in various ways prior to the coming of Christ, so it is simply false that there is something unseemly in thinking about God apart from Christ (Rom 1:20; Heb 1:1–2). Otherwise, the entire Old Testament revelation is unseemly. Moreover, the New Testament

---

1. John of Damascus, *Exposition of the Orthodox Faith*, I.7.
2. Lebens, *Principles of Judaism*, 31.

is quite comfortable talking about the Son existing with the Father prior to creation (John 1:1–3). Jesus even says that he wants humans to experience the kind of love that he and the Father experienced prior to creation (John 17). Hence, the biblical witness itself invites us to reflect on what God is like prior to creation. So I say that we can go right on speculating about what God was like in this precreation state. In fact, I think it will bring us closer to reflecting on what it means for God to be the foundation of reality, and what are God's goals for creating the universe, both of which are important for knowing God well.

What about the suggestion that we don't know enough to really speculate about what God was like prior to creation? This is a legitimate concern as far as it goes, but the fact is that Christian theology is built on the notion of God apart from creation. The oldest time mentioned in the Bible is God's existence prior to creation (Ps 90:2). The New Testament is filled with statements about God's prior existence. This assumes that we can have some grasp of what God is like prior to creation, however limited that grasp may be. In fact, all of the traditional doctrines of God, creation, providence, and incarnation, are built upon speculation into the eternal life of God. So if there is something wrong about such speculation, I am in good company with the rest of Western history in endeavouring to pry into the eternal life of God.

For example, consider the following statement from Boethius.

> Now this our religion which is called Christian and Catholic is founded chiefly on the following assertions. From all eternity, that is, before the world was established, and so before all that is meant by time began, there has existed one divine substance of Father, Son, and Holy Spirit in such wise that we confess the Father God, the Son God, and the Holy Spirit God, and yet not three Gods but one God. . . . The divine nature then, abiding from all eternity and unto all eternity without any change, by the exercise of a will known only to Himself, determined of Himself to form the world, and brought it into being when it was absolutely naught, nor did He produce it from His own substance, lest it should be thought divine by nature, nor did He form it after any model, lest it should be thought that anything had already come into being which helped His will by the existence of an independent nature, and that there should exist something that had not been made by Him and yet existed.[3]

3. Boethius, *Trinity Is One God Not Three Gods*.

Compare a similar statement from the Jewish philosopher Moses Maimonides. He writes, "In the beginning God alone existed, and nothing else."[4] The Islamic philosopher al-Ghazali makes a similar remark. He says that,

> God brought it [the universe] into being after its non-existence, and made it something after it had been nothing, since from eternity He alone was existent and there was nothing along with Him. After that, He originated creation as a manifestation of His power and a realization of what He had previously willed, and of what from eternity had been truly His word. He did this not because of any lack of it or need for it.[5]

The Christian theologian A. W. Pink makes a similar statement as well.

> "In the beginning, God" (Gen. 1:1). There was a time, if "time" it could be called, when God, in the unity of His nature (though subsisting equally in three Divine Persons), dwelt all alone. "In the beginning, God." There was no heaven, where His glory is now particularly manifested. There was no earth to engage His attention. There were no angels to hymn His praises; no universe to be upheld by the word of His power. There was nothing, no one, but God; and *that*, not for a day, a year, or an age, but "from everlasting." During a past eternity, God was alone: self-contained, self-sufficient, in need of nothing.[6]

ON UNNECESSARY PARADOXES

In Boethius, Pink, and many others throughout Western history, there is a clear affirmation that God exists all alone prior to creation. Yet there is something puzzling about these statements. I will point out two puzzles. First, Boethius and Pink claim that God creates time, yet somehow God exists *before* creation. That is puzzling because *before* is a temporal relation, and it makes no sense to say that there is temporality when there is no time. Second, the biblical passages that I cited above speak of God as existing temporally before creation, which contradicts Boethius and Pink's assertion that God creates time with the universe. There are other passages as well, such as Eph 1:4, which explicitly describe God existing before the foundation of the world. Acts 2:23 and Rom 8:29–30 explicitly describe God foreknowing

---

4. Maimonides, *Guide for the Perplexed*, 171.
5. Renard, *Islamic Theological Themes*, 112–13.
6. Pink, *Attributes of God*, 9. Cf. Bates, *Whole Works of the Rev. W. Bates*, 183–85.

and predestining various things. Foreknowledge and predestination are temporal notions that describe God knowing and planning certain events in advance. Second Timothy 1:9 and Jude 25 describe God as existing and doing things before the ages of this world began. Moreover, all of the biblical terms for eternity in the Old and New Testament are temporal words. The Bible knows nothing of timeless existence. All of this seems to imply that time is not created since time already exists before the universe is brought into existence by God. If there is no time prior to creation, then one cannot make the biblical affirmation that God exists *before* creation.

Trying to assert that God exists timelessly before creation is to trade in unnecessary paradox. Allow me to explain what I mean. A paradox is a statement that seems to be a contradiction. In general, it is always best to avoid paradox when one can. If you find yourself asserting seemingly contradictory statements, you ought to do your best to remove the contradiction. That is standard practice in everyday life, and theology is no different. Within the context of theology, an *unnecessary* paradox is when someone asserts an extrabiblical statement that generates a paradox. The case I am asking you to consider at the moment is the assertion that God exists timelessly before creation. The Bible never claims that God is timeless, nor that God exists timelessly before creation. When one asserts that God is timeless before creation, one is asserting an unnecessary paradox.

There is nothing new or original in pointing out that this is a paradox. Theologians have long been aware of this problem. The twentieth-century theologian Emil Brunner asks what was before the universe. He answers, "Before Time there is God Alone."[7] Brunner admits that this is paradoxical, but he tries to remove the paradox by claiming that the *before* is a pre-temporal before.[8] As I see it, this does nothing to remove the paradox. I don't know what a *pre-temporal before* could possibly be. The prefix *pre* implies *before*, thus making the statement look like *before-temporal before*. That is not very illuminating.

The contemporary philosopher William Lane Craig has gone to great lengths to remove the paradox by trying to avoid saying *before* altogether. On Craig's view, God is timeless *without* creation, and temporal *with* creation.[9] Craig has offered a much more rigorous defense of his position than most Christian thinkers. Yet many contemporary philosophers find themselves at a loss for words as to how God's timeless phase of existence could be related to God's temporal phase of existence. It seems like God's timeless

---

7. Brunner, *Christian Doctrine of Creation and Redemption*, 15.
8. Brunner, *Christian Doctrine of Creation and Redemption*, 15.
9. Cf. Craig, *Time and Eternity*.

phase ceases to exist once the universe begins to exist, which would suggest that this timeless phase is not timeless after all.

After reflecting on God's relationship to time in two other books of mine, I have concluded that there is no coherent sense to be found in a pre-temporal before. I also see no point in asserting that God is timeless *sans* creation when it is much more straightforward to assert the biblical affirmation that God exists before creation. If God truly exists alone prior to creation, that is a temporal before. Of course, all of this leads to the question "What is time?" This is a question that most Christian thinkers have tended to avoid answering. I find it less than helpful to avoid that question.

WHAT IS TIME?

This is a perplexing question to address because most discussions confuse different issues. Often, when people talk about time, they are making statements about clocks, or the significance of historical events. None of this answers the question "What is time?" I think it is important to distinguish at least four different kinds of issues. First, what is time? Second, what are moments of time? Third, what moments of time exist? Fourth, what is the significance of a particular ordering of moments or a timeline? I say that a great deal of confusion is introduced in this discussion when these issues are not kept separate.

I start with defining time and moments of time. I take time to be a natured entity that has three roles or functions. Time (i) makes change possible, (ii) is the source of moments, and (iii) is the thing that unifies a series of moments into a timeline. A moment of time is the way things are but could be subsequently otherwise.[10] A moment is a *when* events happen. Moments can be merely possible or actual. A possible moment is a proposition-like entity that describes all of the ways things are but could be subsequently otherwise.[11] An actual moment is when things are in fact a particular way but could be subsequently otherwise. A timeline is a particular coherent successive ordering of possible or actual moments.

This might be difficult to grasp, so I shall try to illustrate the matter. There is a possible moment of you sitting and reading this book. At one moment, you are sitting and reading. At this moment, things could be subsequently otherwise. Why? At the next moment you could put the book down, or keep reading. The way things are is such that they could be subsequently

---

10. Fiocco, "What Is Time?," 56.
11. Byerly, *Mechanics of Divine Foreknowledge and Providence*, 77. Meyer, *Nature of Time*, 59–60.

otherwise at the next moment. There is a vast range of possible moments, and some of these moments can be successively ordered to form a coherent timeline. Consider again the moment of you reading this book. Not just any possible moment can follow from this. Only certain moments can subsequently follow. This is because a moment describes the way things are, and part of the way things are concerns how things have been. At one moment you are reading this book. The next moment cannot be such that you have never read this book. Any moment that might follow from you sitting and reading must be consistent with you having once sat and read this book. This is what I mean by saying that a timeline is a particular coherent successive ordering of moments. A successive series of moments must be consistent. Not just any two moments can be brought together into a timeline.

Before moving on, it is good to clarify something else about timelines. You have probably heard it said that Westerners see time as linear whereas Easterners see time as circular. However, this is a misinterpretation of actual Indian understandings on the nature of time.[12] According to Anindita Niyogi Balslev, this constant slogan that Easterners believe in cyclical time thwarts interreligious communication because it falsely assumes that Judeo-Christian religions have a radically different conception of time from Indo-Hellenic religions.[13] Hinduism, for example, does believe in a pattern of birth, death, and reincarnation, but such events occur successively. One universe comes into existence, and then it is destroyed, and then another universe is brought into existence and so on. These events are all successively ordered into a coherent timeline. As Balslev makes clear, Hindu philosophers had many debates about the nature of time. Is time absolute or relational? Are the moments of time discrete or continuous? Those were questions that were fiercely debated. Yet no one debated if time is actually a circle instead of linear. It was simply assumed that time is linear.[14]

In fact, J. R. Lucas says that no one can actually believe in circular or cyclical time.[15] I agree. When I read biblical scholars or religious scholars talk about time being cyclical, I just think they are confused. What they mean is that certain patterns or types of events seem to repeat themselves. This is what we mean by the often repeated phrase, "Those who fail to learn history are doomed to repeat its mistakes." That is a relatively innocuous claim since certain types of events can be successively repeated. What is outrageous is to say that the exact same events themselves repeat. It is impossible for the

---

12. Balslev, "Time and the Hindu Experience," 170.
13. Balslev, "Time and the Hindu Experience," 176.
14. Balslev, "Time and the Hindu Experience," 177.
15. Lucas, *Treatise on Time and Space*, ch. 9.

exact same event to repeat itself. Any repetition would be a change in the event itself, thus making it a different event. Instead, what we really mean is that a similar type of event has happened before.

Allow me to press on this point a bit more since this is an area of great confusion. Consider the moment of my birth on July 26, 1983. Can that exact same event happen again? If you affirm that the timeline is circular, you must say yes. Things become very absurd very fast at this point. It seems obvious that my birth is before my death. Let's be optimistic and say that I die on July 26, 2083. Further, say that time is circular and that the timeline loops back shortly after my death. If time is circular, my birth is also after my death since July 26, 1983, occurs after July 26, 2083. That sounds implausible, but the implausibility goes deeper. July 26, 1983, is also both before and after itself in the circle of temporal moments. This is so implausible that I see no reason to consider it any further. It is best to stick with what we all know to be true. History is just one damned thing after another, and not some crazy circle.

This brings me to the next issue to consider. What moments of time exist? I affirm a very traditional view called presentism. This view says that only the present moment of time exists, or is actual. Past moments no longer exist as concrete states of affairs. Future moments do not yet exist as concrete realizations of the ways that things could be subsequently otherwise. Most philosophers of time take this to be the common sense, or default view, even if they ultimately do not like presentism. Presentism is incredibly intuitive because it says the present exhausts reality. Whatever exists does so at the present. I don't know about you, but I never find myself existing at any other moment than the present. I never wake up and think, "My goodness, I am in the past!" I do metaphorically say things like, "What is this?! Are we living in medieval times!?" when I encounter something that seems draconian. I also figuratively say, "We are living in the future!" when some new bit of technology is released for public consumers. But such statements are not literal assertions about when I exist, but rather figurative statements about the significance of what is happening right now. Speaking literally, I only ever find myself existing at the present.

Presentism has been the default view for most of history across the world's religions. I am only aware of certain debates among medieval Buddhists where some parties asserted presentism, and others affirmed something called eternalism. On eternalism, all moments of the timeline are fully actual or real. Other than this brief debate, it seems that the majority view has been an implicit presumption of presentism. Yet this commitment to presentism has been questioned in more recent history. In particular, since the advent of the special theory of relativity in the early twentieth century.

On the Minkowski interpretation of special relativity, there is no way to find the present moment. This has led some to say that all moments of the past, present, and future exist. This, however, is quite a leap since there are various ways to find the present moment in contemporary physics. Some of those involve different mathematical interpretations of the special theory of relativity. Despite some different mathematical interpretations, these views are empirically equivalent. Thus leading one to wonder why anyone would favor an interpretation that cannot find something as so obviously apparent as the present moment of time. Other strategies for defending presentism involve noting that the special theory is false since it fails to account for gravity. Gravity is accounted for in the general theory of relativity, and this general theory does have a natural way of finding the present moment. The interpretations of the general theory on which there is a present moment are the ones we use to measure the age of the universe, and thus seem to have a solid credibility, despite the science popularizer's obsession with denying the present. Of course, the general theory of relativity conflicts with most accounts of quantum mechanics, but that should not make one lose confidence in presentism. Among the various accounts of quantum mechanics, there are natural ways to find the present as well. Given this, I find nothing within contemporary physics to shake my confidence in something so incredibly obvious as presentism.[16]

At this point, I have one final issue to discuss before pressing onto the next topic. Far too many discussions about the nature of time conflate time itself with the significance of historical events in time. Often, when some people have a moment of flirting with mysticism, death, or drugs, they will talk about experiences that transcend time itself. They will claim that this mystical experience allows them to see the whole of history all at once, and understand their own place in the world. This might be a religious experience, a near death experience, a political epiphany from a would-be revolutionary, or a drug induced frenzy. As I see it, whatever such experiences are, they are in no way a case of transcending time itself. Nor can such mystical experiences be literally described as timeless.

Recall that a being is timeless if and only if it exists without beginning, without end, without succession, and without temporal location. Anyone who has had a mystical experience or a near death experience does so from a temporal location.[17] You can rightfully ask *when* this person had this experience. In the case of religious experiences, the mystic will often be able to give you the exact date because the experience was so significant to her that

16. For a good introduction to these issues, see Koperski, *Physics of Theism*.
17. Cf. Greyson, *After*, chs. 2–3.

she marked it on her calendar. Hagiographies often note when the mystic had her particular experience, and the significance of this experience for her situation in life. In recent studies on near death experiences, determining when the person in question has died is important to determining that it is a genuine near death experience. All of this involves having a temporal location. Further, these experiences had a beginning, and end, and succession. The experience began at one moment and carried on for long enough for the individual to become aware that something significant is happening. That experience then ended, and she was able to subsequently carry on with the rest of her life. Notice that nothing about this is remotely timeless. However, this is not to say that the experiences are insignificant. It is merely to point out how we often conflate various distinct notions together when we talk about time.

There is time itself, and there are moments of time that can be successively ordered into a timeline. Events happen at moments and over a series of successive moments. Most of what we care about or get passionate about concerns the significance or meaning of those events. Other than the few people like me, most people are not terribly excited about time itself. They are more interested in the meaning of historical events, and where all of this is headed. Is there a purpose in this universe? Why are we here? Why a universe like this? Why did things happen the way that they did? All great questions, but they are not really about time *per se*. They seem to be more appropriately about divine creation and providence. The answers to such questions are found in considering different questions like, "What reasons did God have for creating this particular timeline?" I will return to that question in due course.

GOD AND TIME

That being said, I wish to discuss God's relationship to time. I say that time is an attribute or mode of God. This is because God is a natured entity that (i) makes change possible, (ii) is the source of moments, and (iii) is the thing that unifies a series of moments into a timeline. God has a nature that includes certain essential properties like omnipotence, knowledge, and freedom. Part of what it means to be omnipotent and free is that God has the ability to bring about all manner of states into existence. Freely exercising such power entails undergoing a change and succession because God goes from *having the potential to perform some action* to *actually performing some action*. What this means is that given God's very nature, God is the thing that makes change possible. Moreover, it just follows that there is a way things are but could be subsequently otherwise. God is a being with freedom and maximal power. That is a way things are. Having freedom and power entails the ability to make things subsequently otherwise. So God simply existing with his essential attributes is a way things are but could be subsequently otherwise. Hence, God is the source of the first moment of time by simply existing. God is the source of any subsequent moments by freely exercising his power. Since God is perfectly rational, God always acts for a reason. God will not freely exercise his power unless he does so for a reason. Christian theology claims that God creates the universe according to his wise and sovereign plan. What Christians call divine providence is God's actions to bring about a particular coherent timeline that matches God's plan. Thus, God is a natured entity that makes change possible, is the source of moments, and is the thing that unifies a series of moments into a timeline. God is time!

This may sound shocking since most Christians are familiar with the assertion that God creates time.[18] This is a common Christian claim despite the fact that the Bible consistently describes God being temporal prior to the existence of creation. However, there is precedent within Christian thought for affirming that time is not something to be created, but rather is intrinsic to the divine nature. Such luminaries as Isaac Newton and Samuel Clarke affirmed that time is an essential attribute or mode of God.[19] Various contemporary thinkers like Keith Ward seem to affirm it as well. According to Ward, "There is a divine time, which makes creative change and contingency possible."[20] To be sure, the claim that God is time sounds surprising, but it elicits a greater explanatory power than saying that the timeless and changeless deity somehow magically explains the existence of time and change in the world. How could a timeless being do that? As far as I know, no one has been able to explain how a timeless being can be responsible for the existence of time without immediately running into serious philosophical and theological problems, or punting to ineffable mysteries.[21]

In identifying time with God, I have ruled out divine timelessness. After all, it hardly makes sense to say that time is timeless. That is absurd on its face. Yet, one might wonder if making God temporal is a bad thing. To be honest, I cannot see why it would be bad for God to be temporal.

18. Others might find it shocking because they think that identifying time with God makes God non-personal. If you are tempted to make this muddled inference, I shall ask you to remember that *personhood* is one of God's essential attributes.

19. Cf. Thomas, *Absolute Time*.

20. Ward, *Christ and the Cosmos*, 27.

21. For more on the history of attempts to explain how a timeless being can interact with time, see Mullins, *End of the Timeless God*.

God is eternal in that God exists without beginning and without end. That just follows from God's necessary existence. God is temporal in that God can undergo succession and have temporal location. Is there really anything so troublesome about any of that? God has a temporal location since God exists right now. That hardly sounds like a deeply worrisome assertion. Imagine walking into a church on Sunday and declaring boldly, "Hey everyone! I have come to the most remarkable theological conclusion: God exists right now!" I think you should anticipate some confused looks if you do this. Nothing about saying, "God exists right now" sounds remarkable in the slightest. In fact, you should probably expect a reply like, "Well, yeah! He is omnipresent."

What about succession? Is there a problem with introducing succession into the life of God? Again, it does not really seem that remarkable to say that God does one thing and then another. Anyone who has read the Bible will have noticed that God does one thing and then another. God created the universe. And then, God formed the earth. And then, God created a garden. And then, God. . . . I have not even gotten beyond chapter 2 of Genesis and there is already way too much succession in God's dealings with the universe for him to be timeless. The story of God's interactions with Israel, and his becoming incarnate is all boringly successive. I say *boring* because nothing about the mere fact that God does one thing and then another is terribly interesting. That just follows from God freely exercising his supreme power. Things only become interesting when we consider *what* God has done over the course of history and the significance of those timely events. Of course, things become wildly interesting when I assert that God is time, but that is another story.

As I see it, saying that God is temporal sounds surprising to some, but on closer inspection it is actually a pretty unremarkable notion derived from basic biblical claims about God's interactions with the world throughout history. As such, one should not be worried that there is some deep, troubling difficulty with asserting that God is temporal. Instead, one should find it curious that any Christian who has read their Bible could possibly think that God is timeless.

At this point, someone might ask about the immutability of God since immutability entails timelessness. Doesn't the Bible teach that God cannot change? Again, I find it curious that anyone who has read their Bible could possibly think this. After all, Hosea 11 says that God does change because he is not a stubborn man who lacks compassion!

What is going on here? The traditional doctrine of immutability says that God cannot change in any way, shape, or form.[22] God cannot even change relationally because the immutable and timeless God is not really related to the universe. These are remarkably strong claims, and I don't think that the average Christian understands this. Think of it this way. Can God do one thing and then another? Immutability says no. Can God change from *being angry at your sin* to *forgiving you*? The Bible says yes, but immutability says no. Any kind of change that you can think of, immutability rules out. That looks nothing like what the Bible says about the Christlike God who did not consider divinity a thing to be grasped, and thus took on the form of a servant to save us (Philippians 2). Taking on a human nature is a pretty dramatic change in the life of God.[23]

To be sure, there are passages like Num 23:19, 1 Sam 15:29, and Mal 3:6 that say that God is not a man that he should change his mind. Yet those passages are all very clear in the respect to which God does not change. None of them say that God does not change in any way, shape, or form. In each case, the passages say that men are liars who do not keep their promises. God is not like that. When God makes a promise, he will keep it. His promises are not empty lies. What these passages teach is that the promises of God are trustworthy. They do not teach that God is completely and utterly unchanging. They simply teach that God will not change his mind about the promises that he has made.[24]

Traditional accounts of God's omnipotence and perfect moral goodness factor this in by saying that the almighty God cannot change the past nor undo the promises that he has previously made.[25] Changing the past is logically impossible, and failing to keep a divine promise is morally unacceptable. Thus, it is unthinkable that God would fail to keep his covenantal promises. This is important to keep in view when one is reading Hosea 11. Again, this passage teaches that God does change his mind because he is not a man. The passage is clear that stubborn men who lack compassion will continue down a path of wrath no matter what. Hosea says that God is not like a stubborn man who lacks compassion. God will change his wrath to forgiveness toward his chosen people. Why? God made a covenantal promise toward his people, and he plans on keeping that promise.

---

22. Lombard, *Sentences Book I*, XXXVII.7. Cf. Dolezal, *All That Is In God*, 19.

23. There is a long line of thought within Church history that tries to avoid the incarnation being a change in God. Of course, there is also a long line of thought within Church history of accusing these moves of being the heresy of Nestorianism.

24. Cf. Moberly, *Old Testament Theology*, ch. 4.

25. Wierenga, *Nature of God*, 17. Cf. Aquinas, *Summa Contra Gentiles*, I.83.

THE PRECREATION MOMENT

I now return to the interesting bit: God all alone prior to creation. What was God doing at this precreation moment? There is a very real sense in which God was plotting to take over the world. According to Ephesians 1, before the foundation of the universe, God was devising a plan. This plan involved creating humans for a purpose. That purpose involves humans becoming holy and blameless. Out of love, God created us to be his children through Jesus Christ. When this plan comes to full fruition, God will unite all things together in Christ. That is a pretty amazing plan.

How does God devise this plan? Is this something that he eternally knew he would do, or did God have options? The majority view in Christianity is that God had options, though the details vary about how to describe those options. I will do my best to give you some of the details, starting with what did God know and when did he know it.

There is a somewhat surprising dirty little secret that does not get much attention in contemporary theology. Everyone affirms an open future prior to God's decision to create a universe. It doesn't matter if you are a theological determinist (e.g., a Calvinist), Molinist, or open theist. Branching from the precreation moment are countless possible timelines that God could potentially act to bring about.[26] What this means is that God does not know how the future will in fact unfold. Why? Because God doesn't even know if he will decide to create anything at all at this point, nor has God yet decided what kind of universe he will create. It is fairly standard Christian doctrine that God is free to create or not create. God's choice to create is contingent, not necessary.[27] At the precreation moment, God exists all alone and faces an array of possible universes and timelines that he might bring about. According to T. J. Mawson, "At this stage then, every metaphysical possibility was equally open to Him. Nobody else has ever so fully satisfied the principle of alternate possibilities as God did then."[28]

To be clear, God is not ignorant at the precreation moment. To be ignorant is to be unaware of certain facts. God is omniscient, and infallibly

---

26. Tiessen, "A Response to John Laing's Criticisms of Hypothetical-Knowledge Calvinism," 181. Feinberg, *No One Like Him*, 313. Flint, *Divine Providence*, 46 and 55–57. Rhoda, "Fivefold Openness of the Future." To be sure, the Catholic and Protestant scholastics will try to obscure this dirty little secret by embedding a series of logical moments into a single timeless moment. This is a complicated story, but it entails that from all eternity *God does not know the future* and *God does know the future*. That is a contradiction, and I don't want to let the contradictions of divine timelessness spoil Christian theology any more than they already have.

27. Daeley, "Divine Freedom and Contingency," 563–65.

28. Mawson, "Divine Free Will," 559.

knows all of the facts that there are. There just are no facts about what God himself will do at the precreation moment. Further, God knows all of the possible futures that could obtain if he decides to create anything at all. When God creates, God does not enter into this action blindly. God knows what he is getting into. How?

There is something called the doctrine of divine ideas.[29] The divine ideas are all of the logically possible ways that things could be. The claim is that God's nature or God's mind necessarily emanates all logical possibilities. Perhaps God reflects on his power and intuits all of the things that his maximal power could produce. Alternatively, God's power by itself might entail all of the logical possibilities. I am not terribly interested in taking a stand on precisely how the divine ideas get there. The main takeaway is that all logically possible substances, moments, and timelines are ultimately grounded in the nature of God.

Here is something that the determinist, Molinist, and open theist agree on. In God's precreation moment, all of these views agree that God possesses something called *natural knowledge*. This is God's knowledge of all necessary truths about what is and what could be.[30] At God's precreation moment, God knows all of the possible ways that moments can be ordered by having a perfect grasp of his own essence or nature. Hence, why it is called natural knowledge. God knows all of the logically possible timelines that could obtain. Knowing God's own essence only gives God knowledge of what is possible, or what could take place. God does not know which timeline will in fact obtain because God has not yet decided if he will even create anything at all. Which of those possibilities becomes actual depends on what God freely decides to create if he decides to create anything at all. Once God freely acts to bring about a particular universe, God is said to have something called *free knowledge*. This is God's knowledge of what he has freely done, and of the kind of universe that he has freely brought about.

At this point, I am not ready to offer a discussion on why God creates, nor what kind of universe God creates. I will save that for later chapters. At this stage, I want to discuss the different accounts of God's decrees.

Christians have long reflected on what happens next, though most wish to say that what happens next is still somehow timeless. As should be clear by now, I do not think that God is timeless. Whatever happens next is a new moment in the life of God. What happens next is that God decides that it is a good idea to create something. After that, God considers his options

---

29. Ward, *Divine Ideas*.

30. Goris, "Divine Foreknowledge, Providence, Predestination, and Human Freedom," 111. Molina, *On Divine Foreknowledge*, 130–44.

about what to create, and then decrees that a particular timeline should come about. At this point in the conversation, I shall say a bit about a fairly traditional understanding of the divine decrees. In later chapters, I will take a step back and consider why God would create anything at all, and why God would create a particular universe such as the one we find ourselves in.

THE DIVINE DECREES

As Louis Berkhof points out, it is natural that one should discuss the decrees of God after discussing the essence or nature of God. Now that one knows what God is, one will rightly ask about what God does.[31] Pink draws the connection between God's precreation moment and divine action as follows:

> God was alone when He made His decrees, and His determinations were influenced by no external cause. He was free to decree or not to decree, and to decree one thing and not another. This liberty we must ascribe to Him who is supreme, independent, and sovereign in all His doings.[32]

As I understand it, free will involves the ability to perform an action at the next subsequent moment. What kind of actions can God freely perform at the moment subsequent to his precreation moment? God can perform a creative action. A creative action is when God voluntarily exercises his power to cause a universe to exist.[33] A universe is a collection of contingent beings that are spatiotemporally related to one another. Since God is perfectly rational, God always performs an action for a reason or a purpose. I shall say more about God's reason for creating a universe in later chapters. For now, I wish to emphasize that a perfectly rational God cannot create a universe without having a purpose or plan for that universe. This purpose or plan is referred to as God's decree.

Berkhof says that God's decree is his eternal plan for the created order. The decree to create is not the created universe itself. There is a distinction between the decree and the execution of that decree.[34] Berkhof says that the decree is efficacious and immutable because it is grounded in God's wisdom and omnipotence. Whatever God decrees will certainly come to pass. There can be no sense in which God's decree, or plan, could get screwed up thus

---

31. Berkhof, *Systematic Theology*, 100.
32. Pink, *Attributes of God*, 15.
33. Kraay, *God and the Multiverse*, 4–5.
34. Berkhof, *Systematic Theology*, 103–4.

forcing God to issue a new decree or make changes to his decree at some later time.[35]

What is included in God's decree? As I understand it, God's decree could be general or meticulous. On either view, God's decree will specify a particular goal for creation, but each view differs over how God will providentially achieve that goal. On a general decree, God adopts general-policies for governing the world to that goal. God does not have a specific intention for each and every event that takes place in the history of the universe.[36] On a meticulous decree, God adopts specific-benefit policies for governing the world which would state that every divine act at each moment should achieve a very particular benefit that advances the created universe toward its specific, ultimate end.[37]

In order to understand the difference between these kinds of decrees, it is important to think in terms of whether or not God's decree includes a specific timeline. Calvinists say that God issues a meticulous decree. This means that God freely selects a specific ordering of moments, or a specific timeline. The decree that God issues specifies that a particular universe with a particular timeline will come to exist. God's act of creation brings the universe into existence. In this sense, the decree can be referred to as God's act of predestination since God determines the destiny of all things prior to acting to bring the universe into existence.[38] Subsequent to God's selection of a specific timeline, God is said to have free knowledge. Again, this is God's knowledge of what will in fact occur in the specific timeline that he has freely selected. God has this foreknowledge because of the decree that he freely issued.[39]

Calvinists are quite clear that God cannot foreknow the future unless he causally determines which timeline will occur.[40] On this view, creatures do not have libertarian freedom because God has causally determined which specific timeline will occur. Libertarianism says that freedom is not compatible with causal determinism, whereas compatibilism says that freedom is compatible with causal determinism. Calvinists are usually compatibilists about human freedom, but libertarians about divine freedom.[41]

35. Berkhof, *Systematic Theology*, 104–6.
36. Sanders, *God Who Risks*, 226.
37. Hasker, "Open Theist View," 61.
38. Amyraut, *Amyraut on Predestination*, 60.
39. Berkhof, *Systematic Theology*, 102.
40. Shedd, *Dogmatic Theology*, 394. Cf. Pereboom, "Libertarianism and Theological Determinism," 114.
41. Cf. Daeley, "Divine Freedom and Contingency."

Calvinists typically deny that God can foreknow what creatures will do with libertarian free will.[42] Hence, the only way for God to have exhaustive foreknowledge is if God causally determines everything that will occur. Again, on this view, God issues a meticulous decree. God's providence refers to the execution of that decree to ensure that the details of the decree are fulfilled by either God directly bringing about certain events, or by God indirectly ensuring that creatures bring about certain events.[43] God indirectly brings something about by causing creatures to causally bring about a particular state of affairs.[44]

Molinists wish to affirm that creatures have libertarian freedom, so they add a moment between God's natural and free knowledge. They affirm something called God's *middle knowledge*. This is God's knowledge of counterfactuals of creaturely freedom. Via middle knowledge, God knows what creatures with libertarian freedom would do in any possible circumstance that they might be placed in. God knows this before he issues a decree. On this view, God is able to know all of the possible timelines that he might create, but he is also able to know which timelines are feasible because he knows what creatures would do in each timeline. Molinists say that God uses this middle knowledge to select which universe and which timeline to bring about. On the standard version of Molinism, God issues a meticulous decree because he selects a specific timeline. Thus, God predestines how things will ultimately turn out prior to creation. Subsequent to God's decree, God is said to have free knowledge, and to providentially guide creation to its ultimate goal.[45]

Open theists and Calvinists reject middle knowledge because they think that it is incoherent. They agree that it is impossible for God to know what creatures with libertarian freedom would do, or will do.[46] Yet the open theist parts ways with the Calvinist because the open theist wishes to affirm that creatures have libertarian freedom. In order to preserve creaturely freedom, open theists say that God issues a general decree. The open theist says that prior to God's decree, God knows all of the possible orderings of subsequent temporal moments. Given God's commitment to creating a universe that contains beings with libertarian freedom, it is impossible to know what those creatures will in fact freely do in the future. Hence, there is

42. Turretin, *Institutes of Elenctic Theology*, 212–14.

43. Amyraut, *Amyraut on Predestination*, 59.

44. Webster, "On the Theology of Providence," 164 and 167. Helseth, "God Causes All Things," 31.

45. Flint, *Divine Providence*, 42–43.

46. Berkhof, *Systematic Theology*, 107. Zimmerman, "The A-Theory of Time," 791. Inwagen, "What Does an Omniscient Being Know about the Future?"

no exhaustive timeline that God can decree. Yet, God knows all of the possible actions that his creatures might perform in any possible circumstance within the universe. Prior to the act of creation, God develops an exhaustive contingency plan for every possible future free action in order to guarantee that he achieves his ultimate goal for creation.[47] On open theism, this exhaustive plan to guarantee the achievement of God's goal is predestination.[48] Subsequently, God's act of creation, or decree to create, refers to God willing that a particular universe come to exist. It does not refer to God willing that a particular timeline should come about. Instead, God's decree to create contains a stated goal for the future history of the universe that God intends to providentially bring about in cooperation with his free creatures.

I must emphasize that these are merely the basics for constructing a doctrine of God's decrees. In later chapters, I will develop some of the details. Before that, in the next section, I shall articulate some problems that a model of God must seek to address in order to develop a robust account of the God-world relation that coheres with the standard Christian story.

PROLEGOMENA

Thus far, I have articulated the basics for a doctrine of God and God's decrees. The discussion has raised an assortment of questions related to the doctrines of creation, providence, and human freedom. For the Christian theologian, these topics will also naturally raise the issue of salvation and grace. Here, I will briefly mention some problems to consider, and in subsequent chapters I will explore potential solutions.

Creation Problems. Moses Amyraut states that before one can address the doctrine of predestination, one must answer why God created anything at all, and why God created humans in particular.[49] In contemporary philosophical theology, these are referred to as the General Problem of Creation and the Particular Problem of Creation.[50] These must be addressed be-

---

47. Boyd, "God Limits His Control." For criticism of Boyd's claim that open theism can guarantee God's purposes, see Grossl and Vicens, "Closing the Door on Limited-Risk Open Theism." Other open theists say that God cannot guarantee that his purposes be fulfilled, but the likelihood of divine failure is negligible at best. Rice, *Future of Open Theism*, 231.

48. Despite what I said in the previous footnote, Rice also says that God's predestination guarantees certain outcomes. See Rice, *Future of Open Theism*, 47. That seems to contradict his later statement in his book that God cannot guarantee that his purposes be fulfilled.

49. Amyraut, *Amyraut on Predestination*, chs. 1 and 2.

50. Cf. Kretzmann, "General Problem of Creation."

cause God's reasons for creating will set a goal for the universe. That goal establishes the framework for all of God's subsequent actions in order to achieve that goal or purpose.

Salvation Problems. With regards to human freedom and divine grace, theologians typically affirm the following:

A) Human persons possess the freedom of rational self-determination that is consistent with one's character, judgments, and desires.

B) Human freedom involves the ability to do otherwise at some point in time.

C) God provides efficient grace to the elect to such a degree that the elect willingly cooperate with God's plan of salvation.

A Calvinist like Berkhof says that God's decree is compatible with (A) and (B). God's decree renders future events certain, but it does not deprive humans of their agency. Human persons really could have done otherwise, but it is certain that they will not in fact do otherwise.[51] These are fairly common claims among Calvinists, and are representative of compatibilists more broadly.[52] Calvinists often claim that God's will renders things certain, but does not render them necessary. For example, if God wills that I perform action A at a particular moment of time, then it is certain that I will perform action A at that particular moment.[53] To be sure, Molinists and open theists will deny that a Calvinist can consistently maintain (B), but I shall not explore this issue here.[54]

With regards to (C), Berkhof is clear that God's election of the redeemed is irresistible. He says that human persons can oppose the execution of God's decree to some extent, but that the elect will not ultimately prevail. God influences the elect to make them willing to cooperate with God. However, Berkhof explicitly states that God's influence does not overpower the agency and freedom of the elect.[55] This is a deeply Reformed view.[56] Chapter 3 of the Westminster Confession states that though God ordains all that shall come to pass, God does not do violence to the will of humans, nor does God remove the liberty and contingency of secondary causes. One

---

51. Berkhof, *Systematic Theology*, 107.

52. Couenhoven, *Predestination*, 103–6. Vicens and Kittle, *God and Human Freedom*, 56–57. Crisp, *Deviant Calvinism*, ch. 3. Muller, *Divine Will and Human Choice*.

53. Erickson, *Christian Theology*, 383–84.

54. For a discussion and defense of theological determinism, see Furlong, *Challenges of Divine Determinism*.

55. Berkhof, *Systematic Theology*, 115.

56. Couenhoven, *Predestination*, 105–7.

way to understand this claim is that God offers sufficient grace, and not violent or manipulative grace that completely undermines the freedom of humans. Again, Molinists and open theists will question if a Calvinist can consistently maintain this, but each ought to be happy to affirm that God's grace is not violent nor manipulative.

God's Unfulfilled Desires. A particular problem has plagued Christian theology at various points in history, and it has recently come back in full force. The Bible affirms that Christ offers unlimited atonement. Christ's atonement is not just for a select few, but is said to extend to everyone. Yet, this leads to the problem of God's unfulfilled desires.[57] First Timothy 2:4 says that God desires that all human persons be saved. Second Peter 3:9 says that God is patiently waiting on the final judgment so that all might be saved. Yet, many biblical texts seem to say that not all will repent or be saved (e.g., John 3:18; Heb 10:36; 1 John 2:17; Rev 2:21). It would seem then that God's desire for all to be saved is going to be unfulfilled.

A Christian theologian will need to articulate a model of God and providence that can account for this unfulfilled desire. This is sometimes referred to as hypothetical universalism. God desires that all be saved, but all are not in fact saved. Hence, actual universal salvation does not obtain. A Christian model of God will need to explain why hypothetical universalism, and not actual universalism, is true.[58] In this regard, it will need to specify why it is either impossible or morally impermissible for God to save everyone.[59] Further, a model of God will need to reconcile this with the notion that God's decrees, be they general or specific, cannot fail to obtain.

CONCLUSION

These are the major prolegomena that I shall attempt to address in the following chapters. Along the way, various related problems will pop up, and I will address those as well. Before doing that, however, I need to talk about the consequences of creation for God. If God creates a universe, what are the consequences for him? Christianity proclaims that God has in fact created this universe, so it will be good to explore what the implications are for God's choice to create us. That is what I will discuss in the next chapter.

57. Peckham, *Theodicy of Love*, ch. 2.

58. Unless, of course, you wish to affirm actual universalism. I think that there are compelling arguments in favor of actual universalism. I just find myself uncertain at this moment which view to affirm. In this book, I will try to offer a partial defense of hypothetical universalism.

59. Kronen and Reitan, *God's Final Victory*, 68–71.

4

The Consequences of Creation

ULTIMATELY, I WANT TO discuss the General and Particular Problem of Creation. Before I can discuss those problems, it will be helpful to explore the consequences of creation for God. When God decides to create a universe, there are consequences for God. It is not as if creating an entire universe leaves God completely unchanged. This is the logic of decision.[1] To start, God has changed from not doing anything to doing something. God has also changed from knowing that he exists all alone to knowing that he exists with a bunch of cosmic stuff. Those are genuine changes in the life of God. God cannot freely exercise his creative power without undergoing some kind of change.[2] That is simply what is entailed by the free exercise of creative power. In this chapter, I want to consider some of the other consequences of God's free choice to create. Then, in later chapters I will ask why would God create anything at all, and why would God create a universe like the one we find ourselves in.

LIMITING THE SCOPE OF POSSIBLE ACTIONS

God is free, there is no doubt about that. Yet God's freedom has various limits. Typically, Christians get uncomfortable talking about God facing limits, but it is actually standard theological teaching to say that there are certain logical constraints on God. God's freedom is conditioned by his own necessary existence, for he cannot decide whether or not to exist. God's freedom

---

1. Rice, *Future of Open Theism*, 130.
2. Kittle, "Against Synchronic Free Will."

is conditioned by his own essential nature for God cannot decide whether or not to be God. God's freedom is also conditioned by the necessities of logic and morality.[3] For example, God is perfectly good and thus cannot sin. Part of what it means to be perfectly good is that God cannot sin. In chapter 2, I explained why this is not a problem for God's power and freedom because the ability to sin is a liability and not a power.[4]

Most Christians affirm that there are certain kinds of universes and timelines that God cannot bring about. Since God is perfectly good, God cannot bring about dark timelines in which there is more evil than good, and in which evil is not defeated. For instance, God cannot create a world in which conscious creatures start out in a state of agony that will never be overcome. In this kind of world, conscious creatures are in a perpetual state of suffering that never ceases. Only a terrible person would create a world like that, and God is not a terrible person. As perfectly good, it is impossible for God to create a world like that. Typically, theologians and philosophers say that such a world is metaphysically impossible because a perfectly good being just cannot create such a thing. Thank God for that! Prior to creation, God faces an incredibly large range of possible universes and timelines that he could create, and those universes are ones that are worth creating. Something about these universes is intrinsically good overall even if some of them contain portions of evil and suffering.[5]

Another common logical limit is that God cannot change the past.[6] Once some event is over and done with, that is it. The past is not the sort of thing that one could causally influence. The past is settled, end of story. In reflecting on such claims, Edward Wierenga explains that "at one time God *was* able to bring it about. But he is not able to do so now; it is too late. The moral in this case is that . . . an omnipotent being need not be able to do something that is incompatible with what has already happened."[7] Wierenga connects this with God's moral perfection. A morally perfect God cannot perform any action that goes against his essential moral goodness. If God makes a promise, he cannot fail to keep that promise. To fail to keep his promise would be inconsistent with (i) what has already happened (i.e., God made a promise), and (ii) that God is morally perfect.[8] What this means is

3. Ward, "Cosmos and Kenosis," 164.

4. However, I should note that some argue that God would be greater if he did have the ability to sin. See Howard-Snyder, "Divine Freedom."

5. Cf. Kraay, "Theism, Possible Worlds, and the Multiverse."

6. Bonaventure, *Works of Bonaventure*, 57. Aquinas, *Summa Contra Gentiles*, I.2.25.

7. Wierenga, *Nature of God*, 17.

8. Wierenga, *Nature of God*, 18.

that omnipotence involves God having the power at a particular moment to bring about certain states of affairs at the next moment.

Prior to creation, God faced an open future in which he could causally bring about all manner of possible events. But once God makes a choice to perform a particular action, God cannot undo his act. The scope of God's choices thus shrinks. This shrinkage is not terribly interesting in one sense. This is just the consequence of performing a free action. Imagine God is considering what to create first. Maybe the first thing to create is an angel, or maybe the first thing to create is a single hydrogen atom. Say that God decides to create an angel first before the atom. At that point, God can no longer decide to create the atom first. It is too late to do that because God has already created the angel first. Thus, God's options have shrunk. Of course, the incredible number of options that God has available hardly seem to make this shrinkage a problem for omnipotence. I doubt very much that God will ever run out of subsequent options. My point is merely that the logic of choice entails that certain specific options are ruled out whenever a choice is made.

There are other ways to shrink God's options. If God creates the universe for a particular purpose, then all of God's subsequent actions will be limited by that goal. This is because God's purpose sets the rationale for all of his subsequent actions.[9] Given God's commitment to a particular goal, there will be a rational pattern to the course of actions that God will perform in order to achieve that goal. Theologians have different ways of spelling this out. Some talk about the difference between God's absolute power and his ordained power.[10] God's absolute power is his ability to bring about any logically and metaphysically possible state of affairs. God's ordained power is the actual course of action that God takes in order to achieve his purpose for creation. Once God ordains a particular purpose, it would be irrational for God to act in ways that go against his purposes. God is perfectly rational, and will set an obtainable goal for himself. Whatever that purpose is, God will achieve it through an appropriate course of actions. This does shrink God's options, but that is simply an entailment of God setting a goal that he wants to achieve. I find it implausible that this is a problem for omnipotence since this is merely the consequence of freely exercising omnipotence.[11]

How much shrinkage takes place depends on God's purposes. According to Mawson, if God creates a universe that only contains a single hydrogen atom, then God's options do not shrink that much. God can create an

---

9. Wessling, *Love Divine*, 76.

10. Charnocke, *Several Dischourses upon the Existence and Attributes of God*, 422.

11. Cf. Strong, *Systematic Theology*, 1:286–88. Strong, *Systematic Theology*, 2:371.

atom, make it spin around in the void for a while, and then annihilate it if he wants. There is nothing obviously logically or morally objectionable about any of that. Yet Mawson says that if God creates a universe with morally weighty creatures, then God's options shrink considerably. This is because God acquires particular duties or obligations when he creates beings with moral worth.[12] As perfectly good, God will always fulfill his obligations. Prior to creation, God has no such obligations because there isn't anything else that exists.[13] Once God creates a universe with morally weighty creatures, things change, and God's options shrink.

Not everyone is happy with this. Some philosophers maintain that God does not have any moral obligations toward his creatures.[14] Perhaps God is so great and transcendent that morality just does not apply to him. Personally, I have little taste for these sorts of statements where God is so far beyond us that he looks absolutely nothing like the God revealed through Jesus Christ. The God of the Bible most certainly acquires obligations when he creates a universe and enters into covenantal relationships with his creatures. The God of the Bible makes promises, and thus acquires the obligation of keeping those promises. At least, that is how Old Testament prophets like Malachi see things. The prophets of old are constantly asking God to make good on his covenantal promises. To be sure, some philosophers might argue that God cannot really have obligations since he always, without fail, satisfies his obligations. I think that is just playing with words.

According to C. Stephen Evans, "To be morally obligated to perform an action is to have a powerful reason to perform that action, a reason many would describe as a decisive or overriding one."[15] As Evans sees it, there are certain moral obligations that come with being the creator of the universe, and offering friendship to creatures.[16] I will return to this point in the next section. For now, I shall simply say that the God that Jesus Christ reveals to us is a God who performs morally weighty actions because he has powerful reasons to perform those actions. This is a God who has good reasons to make particular promises to his creatures, and thus freely takes on the obligation of making good on those promises. After all, the Christian faith is standing on the promises of God.

Another consequence of God's free action is that certain values are realized whereas others are not. According to Richard Rice, prior to the act

---

12. Mawson, "Divine Free Will," 559.
13. Mawson, "Divine Free Will," 559.
14. Murphy, *God's Own Ethics*.
15. Evans, *God and Moral Obligation*, 9.
16. Evans, *God and Moral Obligation*, 28.

of creation, God has various options available to him. God could create a world in which absolutely everything is fully determined by God's will, or God could create a universe with an open future in which creatures have a greater degree of power and autonomy. Rice claims,

> It is also important to note that the choice between these options is genuine only if the two worlds are significantly different. A significant choice presupposes genuine alternatives, and real alternatives involve different consequences. After all, not all goods are "compossible," or simultaneously realizable. In choosing between these options, therefore, God embraces the values available in one world but not the other. Either way, God's decision involves a "limitation" of sorts. The values in a divinely determined world are not available in a world where the creatures are free to make undetermined choices. By the same token, the values available in a world where the creatures have the freedom to make such choices would not be available in a world where God's decisions, or decrees, apply to everything that happens.[17]

Part of the logic of making a choice entails that God cannot realize both sets of values. When God creates a universe, God selects one set of values and not another set.

Notice that Rice says these values are not "simultaneously realizable." This again raises the importance of time for theology. Thus far, temporality has been important for articulating divine action. I have spoken about God's inability to change the past, and how each divine action shrinks God's subsequent options. Rice's point here is that certain kinds of values cannot be realized simultaneously or all at once. This does not rule out the possibility of God realizing certain values sequentially. It may be the case that God has created any number of universes prior to our own. Perhaps some universes involved God fully determining everything that happens for a certain amount of time. One possibility is that God created a fully deterministic universe, and decreed that he shall conserve it in existence for seven billion years. After which, God's decree specified that he would create a different kind of universe with a different set of values. I have no idea if God in fact did such a thing. My claim is merely that this is a possibility. The logic of decision rules out certain kinds of values from being simultaneously realized, but it does not rule out certain kinds of values from being sequentially realized.

17. Rice, *Future of Open Theism*, 130–31.

THE PERSONAL CONSEQUENCES OF DIVINE ACTION

At this point, I want to consider the consequences of divine action for God's personal life. Thus far I have outlined how God's actions shrink the range of subsequent actions that God can and will perform. What about the more personal consequences? How does any of this impact God's personal life.

As alluded to earlier, God's knowledge will change when he makes a decision. Prior to the act of creation, Calvinists, Molinists, and open theists agree that God faces an open future. God does not know what he himself will do. When God decides to create, his knowledge will track his decision.[18] God's knowledge will correspond to whatever choice he has made, and will track the consequences of that choice. If God creates a Calvinist or a Molinist universe, then the consequence is that God will have exhaustive foreknowledge of what will take place in that universe. If God creates an open universe, then the consequence is that God will have an exhaustive knowledge of all the possible and probable timelines that could follow from that divine decision. Whatever God freely decides to do, what God knows will change.[19] Otherwise, God would not be omniscient.

This kind of knowledge that I have spoken of is merely propositional. God's knowledge changes in other respects as well. God's experiential knowledge will change. There is something that it is like to create a universe. This kind of experiential knowledge cannot be had without creating a universe. Some might complain that the omniscient God must be able to know such things prior to creation, but I say this is nonsense. It is one thing to imagine what the experience is like, and it is another to actually experience it. Perhaps the divine ideas give God a superior kind of experiential knowledge in which God can imagine or simulate what it is like to create a universe. However, experiential knowledge of a simulation is experiential knowledge of a simulation. It is not the same thing as experiential knowledge of actually creating a universe. A cognitively excellent God can tell the difference. Thus, when God creates a universe, God has a new experience and acquires new experiential knowledge.

Another important consequence of freely creating a universe pertains to God's emotions. God's emotional life will be impacted by the kind of universe that he makes. If God freely decides to create a universe with morally weighty creatures, this has consequences for the kind of emotions God will have. God has decided to create a universe with human persons that he will love for all eternity. Part of what it means for God to love humans

---

18. Sanders, *God Who Risks*, 15.
19. Ward, *Christian Idea of God*, 149–50.

is that God values their existence and flourishing, and God values having a union or friendship with humans.[20] Valuing something, or caring about something, creates a disposition to have certain kinds of emotions toward that thing. If you care about something, you deem that thing to be worthy of your attention and worthy of you to act on behalf of it. An emotion is a felt evaluation of some object or circumstance that is grounded in one's own cares and concerns. If God creates a universe with things that are valuable, God will acquire certain stable dispositions or sentiments toward those valuable things. This is because God deems these objects to be worthy of his attention and action. This concern toward his creatures and his plans for those creatures grounds a range of possible emotions that God can have.

To be sure, the classical Christian tradition claimed that God is always in a state of pure, undisturbed bliss. They said that it is impossible for God to be moved, influenced, or impacted by creatures in any way. In fact, God's emotions are always and only about himself. But this is so far removed from the Christlike God that one should question if this is even a Christian conception of God. When one reads the Bible, God is often compared to a parent or a spouse who has strong affections toward his beloved. God is emotionally invested in his creatures because he deems them to be worthy of his attention and action. God takes pleasure in his creatures, but God is also perturbed by their sinful actions. This is what we should expect of a perfectly moral and rational God.

Yet the classical Christian tradition disagrees with the biblical portrayal of God. Classical Christian theism says that it is impossible for God to suffer in the divine nature. Despite overwhelming evidence in the Old Testament that God suffers, the classical theist says that it is impossible for God to suffer.[21] Instead, God is necessarily in a state of pure, undisturbable happiness or bliss. However, some theologians and philosophers think that it would be immoral if God did not suffer with his creatures. There is something unseemly about God knowingly creating a universe with inevitable suffering, and yet knowing full well that he will remain in a state of pure bliss throughout. There are no consequences for God's actions in this picture of the world. Create a universe with a great deal of misery, or create a universe with creatures hooked up to a pleasure machine, or don't create anything at all. Nothing really matters to the classical God either way. God is completely unaffected by creation. He remains in a state of pure bliss, yet asks his creatures to suffer. Something just seems morally off about a God like that.

20. Wessling, *Love Divine*, 54.
21. Cf. Fretheim, *Suffering of God*.

It is difficult for me to pin down exactly what is morally off about a God like this, but I can explain some of my intuitions. Consider a person named Monica who has lived her entire life in the lap of luxury. She has never suffered in any significant way, except for the occasional frustration of her servants failing to satisfy her every whim. A person like Monica does not understand the weight of suffering. If she commands that her servants perform some miserable task that she herself is unwilling to perform, she simply cannot understand the pain that she is inflicting upon them. There are several things morally off about Monica. To start, she lacks the relevant moral knowledge of what she is asking of her servants. Also, she seems to lack any real care about the well-being of her servants.

When it comes to the classical God, one might say that the case of Monica is not analogous to God. Perhaps a classical theist will say that God is omniscient, so God cannot lack any relevant moral knowledge. A classical theist might also say that God has a great deal of care and concern for his creatures and their well-being. Yet I say that the classical theist cannot consistently maintain this. It is difficult to maintain that God has the relevant moral knowledge of pain and suffering when it is metaphysically impossible for God to suffer. Sure, God knows all of the propositions that describe pain and suffering, but such a being does not understand the phenomenology of suffering. A necessarily happy God cannot possibly grasp the weight of pain precisely because he knows nothing but pure bliss. As far as I can tell, God's undisturbed happiness prevents God from having access to morally relevant knowledge.

Further, the classical tradition is quite explicit that God's primary cares and concerns can only be himself. All of God's actions are for his own glory or goodness. All of God's love is self-love. The consistent classical theist will have a difficult time explaining how God actually has cares and concerns toward his creatures precisely because she says that God is completely unmoved and uninfluenced by anything outside of himself. Many contemporary thinkers seem to be under the impression that God just automatically has cares and concerns for his creatures, but this is deeply mistaken. Consider the classical thinker Augustine, who struggled to maintain a satisfying account of God's love for creatures since God's love is only ever self-love. For Augustine, God can either enjoy creation or use creation. On Augustine's understanding, to enjoy something for its own sake is to properly love that thing. To use something is an improper form of love. So Augustine is asking if God can properly or improperly love creation. Augustine says that God cannot enjoy creation since the only thing worthy of enjoyment is himself. That would seem to leave God's only option as using creation. Yet even here, Augustine fudges. He points out that God cannot have any use for creation.

A God who is perfect in bliss and goodness cannot possibly have a use for anything, according to Augustine.[22] In light of that, I fail to see how God could possibly have any cares or concerns for his creatures. They are not even of any possible use to him so God cannot even improperly love them. Again, I say that there is something morally off about a God like this.

As I see it, a perfectly good God will be emotionally impacted by his creation. Richard Swinburne maintains that if God makes a universe in which creatures suffer, then his perfect goodness would lead him to share in our suffering. As perfectly good, God will always perform a best action if there is one. If there is no best action, then God will perform an action that advances his purposes. In this case, Swinburne thinks that there is a best action to perform, and that action is for God to suffer with his creatures. In fact, Swinburne thinks that God must become incarnate and share the suffering with his creatures.[23]

Others share Swinburne's views on this point. Francis McConnell thinks that the consequences of a morally perfect God's creative act are clear. He writes,

> God is under heavy moral obligations to come near his children in the very deepest sense possible. He has sent his children forth into a terribly painful world, and he must do all he can to render the pain tolerable. He has bestowed upon men the unsolicited boon of freedom—an awful gift—and he is thereby under moral necessity to go to extremes to relieve men from the evil which thus becomes almost inevitable. If God is a moral God we have in the infinite intensity of his ethical life a mighty pressure which sends him towards the lots of his children. We may speak of this center of power as the conscience of God—to use a term which will suggest an unresting insistence. . . . The Father is under unescapable responsibility for the welfare of his children.[24]

For McConnell, the incarnation of God is the outcome of God trying to satisfy this obligation. He says that God "is really anxious to show us that our shoulders are not weighted with any burden which he is not willing so far as possible to take upon himself."[25] God comes to know the loneliness of physical helplessness, and the pathway to death. For McConnell, "the Cross shows us a Father under moral obligation to exert every moral influence

---

22. Oord, *Pluriform Love*, ch. 5.
23. Swinburne, *Existence of God*, 264–65.
24. McConnell, *Divine Immanence*, 96–97.
25. McConnell, *Divine Immanence*, 108.

for the moral salvation of his children."[26] Yet, he does not think that the salvation of mankind is the primary function of the incarnation and Christ's death on the cross. As McConnell explains,

> The Cross is, first of all, God's supreme satisfaction of his own conscience, the preservation of his own self-respect. God has sent men forth into a terrible universe without consulting them, and has thrust into their hands the awful boon of freedom. He is thus under enormous moral obligation. He need not have created men, but having created them he cannot discharge his moral bonds to them and to himself short of Calvary. There is no responsibility in the universe so heavy as that of Creatorship. If the Biblical teaching, that the earthly pain of man is in part at least a consequent of moral evil, has within it a grain of truth it is hard to see how a moral Creator could have peace of conscience without sharing the pain made necessary by the moral imperfections flowing from an unsolicited gift of freedom.[27]

I find this suggestion quite plausible. Something is morally suspect about a God who creates a universe with a kind of suffering that he himself is unwilling to endure. As I will discuss in later chapters, every view of providence affirms that sin, evil, and suffering are inevitable in the kind of universe that God selects to create. If God creates a universe knowing that suffering is inevitable, and God is unwilling to suffer along with his creatures, then God seems to be asking something utterly outrageous of his creatures. God would be commanding us to participate in his creative project without putting any skin in the game. That seems wrong. It would suggest that the lives of his creatures have no personal impact on him. Instead, a morally good God will not ask his creatures to endure a kind of suffering that he himself is unwilling to endure. A morally good God will demonstrate to his creatures that his creative project is worth it by becoming incarnate, and enduring the kinds of trials that he asks us to endure. As I see it, the incarnation is in part a demonstration that God is willing to put some skin in the game in order to see his creative project through to the end. Thus the act of creating a universe has significant personal consequences for God.

THE HAPPINESS OF GOD

For McConnell and many others, God's creative act entails that God acquires particular moral obligations toward his creatures. As perfectly moral

26. McConnell, *Divine Immanence*, 111.
27. McConnell, *Divine Immanence*, 109–10.

and rational, God's emotional life is impacted by the kind of world that he creates. There are consequences for his actions, and God is more than willing to accept those consequences for the sake of achieving his ultimate purposes. This means that God is not always going to be in a state of pure bliss. God will be as happy as it is morally and rationally appropriate to be in any given circumstance, but there are many circumstances in which God will be in a state that is less than pure felicity.

In order to understand this point, it will be helpful to briefly reflect on the nature of happiness. What is happiness? Typically, one might think that happiness is feeling good. That is certainly one factor in happiness.[28] Yet the history of philosophical reflection has often said that happiness requires a great deal more. For example, a common theme is that happiness involves considering how all of a person's intended goals come together to form a plan that is eventually completed.[29] For many philosophers, this is not mere desire satisfaction because genuine, lasting happiness must have moral goods in the intended goals. The way that one articulates goodness, well-being, and other moral concepts will condition the way that one articulates what exactly it means to be happy. Yet the big idea is that there is some sort of harmony between one's goals, the nature of reality, and the ultimate good.[30]

In a similar vein, Robert C. Roberts points out, "Happiness is more than feeling good. It is a matter of attunement to oneself and to one's world; of acting well whether or not with pleasure; of good personal relationships even if they are sometimes painful and seem unsatisfying."[31] As Roberts understands things, happiness is about being attuned with one's nature and with the nature of the universe. This is distinct from what he calls circumstantial attunement, or satisfaction. I'll start with circumstantial attunement. You may very well be having pleasurable experiences in your current circumstance, but that is not necessarily happiness. The drug addict who is experiencing a high is certainly in the circumstance of being satisfied, but this is hardly happiness. New parents may very well experience displeasure in the circumstance of a crying baby waking them in the middle of the night, but that does not necessarily mean that the parents are unhappy.

According to Roberts, happiness ideally will involve both metaphysical attunement and circumstantial attunement. What is metaphysical attunement? Roberts says, "This attunement occurs when one cares about what

---

28. Roberts, *Emotions in the Moral Life*, 164.
29. White, *Brief History of Happiness*, 10–14.
30. White, *Brief History of Happiness*, 32–36.
31. Roberts, *Emotions in the Moral Life*, 158.

is really important, by the lights of one's metaphysics, and the depth of one's cares is keyed both to the import and to the particular value—goodness or badness—of things."[32] Here is the big idea. Think about what really matters, or what is truly good. Do your cares and concerns line up with those things? If the answer is yes, then you are metaphysically attuned to the way the world is. Your emotions will properly track what is going on in the world. Return to the example of the new parents. To be sure, waking up to the sound of a crying baby is less than pleasant. The parents will be experiencing circumstantial dissatisfaction. But the parents have an appropriate concern for the baby and its well-being. Their metaphysical attunement involves valuing the existence and flourishing of the child. It also involves valuing the development of a meaningful relationship with their child. The parents will develop plans to help their child flourish, and plans to develop a lasting relationship with their child. In light of this, some temporary dissatisfaction seems worth it. While their circumstantial happiness may be diminished, their overall metaphysical attunement remains intact. Genuine happiness will be fulfilled as the parents see their goals for their child achieved.

Let's get back to God's happiness. According to Brian Leftow, "Moral perfection is a matter of attitudes and of habits of action, thought, emotion, and will." Leftow takes this to be a consequence of God's perfect rationality.[33] Leftow draws out some of the consequences for God's happiness. He writes,

> The Bible calls God blessed or happy (1 Timothy 1:11, 6:15). It does not say that He is perfectly so. If God is perfectly rational, He has *inter alia* a concern for His own happiness. If He is omniscient, omnipotent. . . . He can maximize His own happiness come what may. A rational being would not let Himself be less happy than He could be in His circumstances if He had the choice. Given God's powers and opportunities, He always has the choice.[34]

God has made the choice to create a world with morally weighty creatures with the goal of entering into genuine loving friendship. As such, God is emotionally invested in the flourishing of these creatures, and emotionally invested in achieving friendship with these creatures. If God were not emotionally invested, then his providential and salvific actions make no sense. Bertrand Brasnett goes further in saying that this would be downright irrational and immoral. For Brasnett, it is difficult to think that God is indifferent to sin that violates his ultimate purposes for creation. If God

---

32. Roberts, *Emotions in the Moral Life*, 165.
33. Leftow, *God and Necessity*, 8.
34. Leftow, *God and Necessity*, 9.

66   THE CONSEQUENCES OF CREATION

is unconcerned when his will is disobeyed, then Brasnett thinks that God would be false to himself. God would not be a truly moral being. He further writes, "A God who could create a universe that his will might be done therein, and then be supremely indifferent when that will was disregarded, would indeed be a strange being devoid of rationality."[35]

If God does not care about his creatures, then he would not deem them worthy of his attention and action. As it stands, the God of the Bible has revealed himself as morally and emotionally invested in his creation. He deems the universe to be worthy of his attention and action. God freely accepts the consequences that this has for his emotional life.

For Leftow,

> God's moral nature imposes on Him perfect moral reactions: if what creatures suffer and do ought to lower His happiness, it does, and lowers it as much as it should. Maximal happiness would not be an admirable property if it were not morally appropriate to have it. The property God has, I suggest, is this: He is such as always to have the maximum morally permissible happiness.[36]

To be clear, when God decides to create a universe like the one we find ourselves in, God is giving up a state of pure bliss. Prior to creation, Keith Ward says that God is "supremely happy in the contemplation of a huge array" of divine ideas.[37] Though Ward says that our ability to imagine God's bliss is beyond our ken, Ward is clear that God enjoys a state of blessedness as he contemplates all of the logical and metaphysical possibilities.[38] William Hasker agrees. Prior to creation, the life of the triune God is completely satisfying. God has no need to create a universe in order to be satisfied.[39] For Hasker, it is a matter of wonder and amazement that God would give this up and accept the cost of divine suffering by creating a world like this.[40]

God deems it to be worthwhile to give up this state of pure bliss in order to achieve his purposes for creation. God freely accepts the suffering that comes with creating a universe like ours. Yet it should not be thought

---

35. Brasnett, *Suffering of the Impassible God*, 8. Brasnett is taking direct aim at the doctrine of impassibility which says that God is not impacted by sin. As the proponent of impassibility James E. Dolezal affirms, "Our sins, be they ever so many, have no effect on God." Dolezal, "Strong Impassibility," 23.

36. Leftow, *God and Necessity*, 9.

37. Ward, *Christian Idea of God*, 127.

38. Ward, *Christian Idea of God*, 130.

39. Hasker, *Providence, Evil, and the Openness of God*, 182.

40. Hasker, *Providence, Evil, and the Openness of God*, 183.

that God is in a state of pure agony as he sustains the universe in existence. Nor should we think that God's emotional life is entirely dependent upon us mere mortals. God loves us humans, but not everything is about us. God can empathize with a wide range of our experiences, but this does not entirely dictate which emotions God will have. According to Ward, God will know what it is like for you be happy, to be sad, and so on, but there are certain emotions that God cannot have. For example, sometimes in our suffering we find ourselves completely overwhelmed. We might judge life to be pointless. Ward says that God knows what it is like for us to feel like life is pointless. "But God will never actually experience that life is pointless."[41] Why? Because God knows that life is not actually pointless. Through empathy, God knows what it is like for you to lose all hope, but God's own emotional evaluation of the situation will not be one of utter hopelessness. This is because God knows that his providential actions will ultimately bring about his desired purposes for creation.

One significant consequence of God's free choice to create a universe like this is that God must give up a state of pure bliss. However, we should not think of this as a permanent consequence of God's free action. According to Ward, this state of bliss is something that God freely gave up in the gracious act of creation for a limited time.[42] God is "a passionate mind who sacrifices divine beatitude in order to relate to created minds."[43] God gives up unadulterated bliss in order to bring about new values that would not exist otherwise. In particular, the value of creator-creature friendships. As Ward writes,

> God shares in the pain and permits the wayward freedom of creatures in order that, finally, creatures should share in the bliss and become vehicles of the truly creative freedom of the divine nature. It is that cosmic movement from divine self-emptying to creaturely fulfilment in God which is the spiritual history of the cosmos, and, it seems to me, it is also the deepest meaning of the Christian Gospel for this planet in the middle of its journey through the mystery of time.[44]

God is only experiencing suffering for a limited time as he engages in the redemptive work of creation. Once God's redemptive work is complete, the eschatological wedding feast can be fully enjoyed by God and creatures. As McConnell explains, God and creatures share in the cross-bearing

41. Ward, *Christian Idea of God*, 174.
42. Ward, "Cosmos and Kenosis," 157.
43. Ward, *Christian Idea of God*, 191.
44. Ward, *Christian Idea of God*, 203.

suffering that brings about a deep unity of love between God and humanity. This cross-bearing suffering will eventually give way to a joy and peace that shall never end. McConnell says that the "pain is not the lasting phase of feeling, but joy. Joy abideth. Peace remaineth. The joy and peace that endure take their start from fellowship in sorrow."[45]

CONCLUSION

When God decided to create a universe, he knew what the consequences would be. Our gracious and loving God considered those to be acceptable consequences. That might be difficult to fathom, but I want to explore that in the next few chapters. In order to get a partial grasp on why God would consider these consequences to be acceptable, I need to ask why God would create anything at all, and why God would create a universe like the one that we find ourselves in.

---

45. McConnell, *Is God Limited?*, 293.

5

Why Create Anything at All?

As I said before, if you want to be close to God, you will need to know what God is like, what God cares about, and what God's goals are. Thus far, I have been primarily focusing on what God is like, only making suggestions about what God cares about and what God's goals are. In these next few chapters, I want to dive deeper into God's goals. In chapter 3, I introduced the idea of God's decree, or predestination. Moses Amyraut states that before one can address the doctrine of predestination, one must answer why God created anything at all, and why God created humans in particular.[1] In contemporary philosophical theology, these are referred to as the General Problem of Creation and the Particular Problem of Creation.[2] In this chapter, there are three primary questions that I want to answer. (1) What are the General and Particular problems of creation? (2) Why does it matter that God has a reason for creating a universe? (3) Why create anything at all?

THE GENERAL AND PARTICULAR PROBLEM OF CREATION

The General Problem of Creation is a family of arguments which attempt to demonstrate that God has no reason to create anything at all. This is a serious problem that is often overlooked in contemporary theology. Most

---

1. Amyraut, *Amyraut on Predestination*, chs. 1 and 2.
2. Cf. Kretzmann, "General Problem of Creation," and Kretzmann, "Particular Problem of Creation."

people just assume that God had a perfectly good reason to create, but they often do not consider if that reason is consistent with their conception of God. As I have argued elsewhere, various classical claims about God are inconsistent with God having any reason to create at all. In which case, any creative act by God would be utterly arbitrary. That is not consistent with God's perfect rationality.[3] Medieval Jaina philosophers offered a twist on this argument. They would say that God has no good reason to create anything at all. From there, they argued that one cannot infer the existence of God from the existence and nature of the universe. In other words, the General Problem of Creation can be used to undermine cosmological and design arguments for the existence of God.[4]

To illustrate this problem, I want to return to Amyraut. With regards to the General Problem of Creation, Amyraut seems to give a fairly classical answer. He says that God's principal reason for creating is his own goodness.[5] Yet, there is a potential ambiguity in Amyraut's thinking. What does it mean for God to create for his own goodness? Sometimes people say that this means that God creates for his own glory. Amyraut is clear that God's reason for creating is not so that God might acquire glory. God already has all glory, and creating a universe can add no further glory to him. Yet Amyraut seems to offer several different principal reasons for God's act of creation. On one occasion, he says that God's principal reason in creating a universe is so that God can exercise his attributes, such as his goodness.[6] On another occasion, Amyraut says that God's principal reason in creating a universe is so that God's goodness might be revealed in nature.[7] It is not clear how these seemingly different reasons fit together. Ambiguities like these in Amyraut's writings are one reason that he was criticized by his contemporary Reformed theologians, though these sorts of ambiguities about God's reasons for creating are ubiquitous in Christian theology.

It is far from obvious that Amyraut has answered the General Problem of Creation. As Paul Helm argues, God is essentially good, and thus God's goodness cannot serve as a reason to create because God's goodness would be exactly the same if he creates or does not create.[8] In order to understand this problem, consider the classical distinction between God's immanent and transitive acts. God's immanent acts are necessary and toward himself,

---

3. Mullins, "Problem of Arbitrary Creation for Impassibility."
4. Bossche, "Jain Arguments Against Nyaya Theism."
5. Amyraut, *Amyraut on Predestination*, 67.
6. Amyraut, *Amyraut on Predestination*, 66.
7. Amyraut, *Amyraut on Predestination*, 68.
8. Helm, *Eternal God*, 176.

whereas his transitive acts are contingent and toward others. Immanent actions are classically said to be actions within the Trinity apart from creation. Transitive actions are classically said to be actions like creation, providence, and salvation.

Hence, when classical thinkers say that God's reason for creating is "to will his own good," they have run afoul of their own distinction between immanent and transitive acts. God necessarily wills his own good, thus making it an immanent act. Moreover, willing his own good is quite clearly an act directed toward himself and not others, thus making it an immanent act. What is needed is a reason to perform a contingent, transitive act of creating a universe. Something that God necessarily does toward himself cannot provide a reason for a contingent act directed toward others.

That is the General Problem of Creation. Now I need to say something about the Particular Problem of Creation. The Particular Problem of Creation asks about the reasons for why God would create one particular universe over any other. The worry here is about another potential conflict with God's perfect rationality. If God does not have a sufficient reason to create one universe over another, then it might seem like God is acting arbitrarily. Yet a perfectly rational God cannot act arbitrarily.

With regards to the Particular Problem of Creation, Amyraut is more interested in why God created human persons. At best, this would only give us a partial answer to the Particular Problem of Creation, which is concerned with why God created this universe rather than another. Amyraut says that God created human persons so that they can bear his image. Amyraut has two things in mind with regards to image bearing: goodness and happiness. Amyraut affirms that God is by nature perfectly good and happy. Further, he takes moral goodness to be a prerequisite for happiness. Thus, in order for humans to be happy, they must first be morally good. In order for humans to be good, God has given humans the cognitive faculties of understanding, reason, and wisdom, and God has placed them in a universe in which they can cultivate these faculties in order to obtain goodness.[9] In order for God to satisfy his goal of creating good and happy creatures, God will need to have a wise plan for the future that he can providentially execute over the course of history.

---

9. Amyraut, *Amyraut on Predestination*, 69–72.

WHY DO GOD'S REASONS MATTER? THE IMPORTANCE OF GOD'S PERFECT RATIONALITY

One of the aims of this book is to offer some reflections on the divine attributes and how they impact other areas of doctrine and spiritual practice. Perfect rationality is an essential divine attribute. God is perfectly rational if God always acts for a reason. This might sound kind of abstract, and not immediately inspire any sort of praise toward God. Yet God's rationality is something that is assumed in standard Christian discourse, and serves as a basis for trusting God. Think about how often Christians speak of God's wise and loving plan for our lives. Statements about God's wise plan are assuming God's perfect rationality. In fact, God's perfect rationality is assumed in most areas of Christian doctrine, so there is a very pressing sense in which the system of Christian belief hangs on this divine attribute. I will offer some examples of this before explaining the significance for our personal lives.

First, consider the issues of theodicy and the problem of evil. There are several different kinds of questions that theologians try to address when articulating a theodicy, or a justification for why God permits evil. To start, why is there all of this evil and suffering in the world? Theologians will claim that God has good reason to allow the kinds of evil and suffering that we see in the world. One common answer is that God gave humans freedom so that they can develop their moral character. There are other kinds of answers one can give, but my point is that an answer to this question posits a reason for why God acts in the ways that he does. Why say that God has a good reason to allow evil? The answer is rather simple. If God had no good reason to allow all of this suffering, then God does not seem like a very good person. Good people act for objectively good reasons. If God has no reason at all for allowing suffering, it is very difficult to say that God is good or that God cares about us.

Second, when it comes to the Christian doctrine of salvation, another kind of question arises. What is wrong with humanity? Christian theologians will often start talking about sin at this point before moving on to discuss Christ's atoning life and death. This leads to several other questions that have occupied theologians for centuries. Why did God the Son become incarnate? Why did the Son have to die on a cross? How does any of this actually save me? These are all great questions, though I have nothing terribly interesting to say about them here. I raise these questions to point out the role of divine rationality in answering these questions. When theologians attempt to answer these questions, they offer reasons for why God became incarnate and died for us. They appeal to biblical passages about God's plan

WHY CREATE ANYTHING AT ALL? 73

to save the world through Christ. Basically, God had good reason to become incarnate and die for humanity. Whichever way one develops a doctrine of salvation, one will be positing some kind of reason for why God did what he did. Some will say that an incarnation and atoning death is the only way that God could save us. Others claim that God could have saved us in many other ways, but that an incarnation and atoning death is the best or most fitting way to accomplish the goal of saving humans. Either way, the Christian understanding of incarnation and salvation depends on God's perfect rationality.

Third, there are other areas of Christian doctrine where God's perfect rationality is assumed. Consider the doctrines of predestination and election. Prior to creation, God is said to develop a wise and loving plan or a destiny for humanity. When we say that God develops a wise and loving plan, we are presupposing that God has a good reason for this particular plan. God's plan cannot be wise if it is not grounded in objectively good reasons. Terrible plans are based on terrible reasons, and we do not typically say that people who implement terrible plans are wise. Nor do we want to put our trust in people who implement terrible plans. Whichever way you want to develop the doctrine of predestination, it will be assuming God's perfect rationality. The same goes for election. On some accounts of predestination, God is said to elect who will be saved and who will be damned before he creates the universe. For some, this is a hard pill to swallow. They ask how God could decide to damn someone before that person even comes into existence. For those who defend this account of election, they reply that God has a good reason for his choice of who to elect. Sometimes theologians get pushed into a corner because they find all of the possible reasons for God to damn someone prior to their birth otiose. In these cases, theologians usually punt to "God's hidden will." This is a phrase that refers to God's reason for damning someone in advance, but that reason is hidden from humanity. On this view, we are told that God definitely has a good reason to damn people in advance, but we just don't know what that reason could be.[10] Regardless of whether or not you find this plausible, notice that the theologian is demonstrating a commitment to God's perfect rationality. They are unwilling to say that God just damns people on a whim. Why? Because good people do not damn others to eternal conscious torment for no reason.

Thus far, I have pointed out several areas of systematic theology where God's perfect rationality is assumed. By and large, theologians have been

---

10. As the Calvinist Paul Helm makes clear, God's actions are never capricious or arbitrary. Helm, *Providence of God*, 34.

unwilling to say that God acts arbitrarily when it comes to the existence of evil, the salvation and ultimate destiny of humanity, and the incarnation. Oddly, however, some Christian theologians have faltered when it comes to the doctrine of creation. Why did God create anything at all? Most theologians try to think of a reason for why God created, but various other doctrines like impassibility prevented Christians from giving satisfying answers. Thus leading to an arbitrary creation where God has no reason to create at all.[11] Here is a question to consider at this point. Does it matter if God has no reason to create? I say that it matters quite a lot.

First, if you say that God has no reason to create, then you are abandoning God's perfect rationality, and denying that God created the universe through wisdom (Prov 3:19–20). You will have to say that God is not a perfectly rational being. Without God's perfect rationality, you will need to rethink your approach to theodicy, salvation, incarnation, predestination, and election. Earlier, I noted how various accounts of these topics assume that God must be acting for an objectively good reason. Yet, without perfect rationality, one can address all of these topics in a radically different way. This is because you are no longer constrained in the kinds of answers that you can give once you are freed from the need to posit that God acts for a reason. Consider how one might answer the previous theological questions once one is freed from the shackles of perfect rationality.

> A No Reason Theology: Why does God allow evil? Perhaps God just does for no reason. Why did God the Father send Jesus to the cross? For no reason. Why does God develop a plan for human destiny? No reason. Why does God damn some and save others? No reason.

Pause and reflect on this for a moment. Does that really sound like a being worthy of worship? Does that sound like a perfectly good and loving being? Hardly. Imagine leading a group of people in the following prayer. "God, we want to praise you for the arbitrary actions that you have performed. According to your non-rational counsel, you have created us for no reason, and eternally damned many on a whim. Oh great and holy One, for no reason whatsoever, you sent your Son to die on our behalf when there were many other options available. According to your great plan, you have allowed us to suffer gratuitously. Hallowed be Thy Name!" That sounds absurd on its face. It looks as if throwing out God's perfect rationality sinks the entire plausibility of Christianity.

---

11. Mullins, "Problem of Arbitrary Creation for Impassibility."

It will do no good to reply that though God is not perfectly rational, God can sometimes act rationally. The reason why this is not helpful is because we can ask why God acts rational only sometimes. We can do this to some extent with humans, but it is difficult to apply this to God. We can point out that humans act on unconscious impulses, but that does not seem right for divine action. What kind of answer could one give for why God acts rationally sometimes and arbitrarily other times? Perhaps one could say, "God just felt like acting rationally today, though he has no reason to act rationally." That hardly seems like a perfect being.

Though, it is worth pointing out that God may sometimes act in ways that I call *nested arbitrary actions*. As Sam Lebens explains, God always acts for a reason unless God has a good reason not to.[12] Nested arbitrary actions are actions that seem arbitrary in isolation, but are not arbitrary when considered in the wider context of an agent's goals. Consider cases where you are hungry, and you are confronted with two equally delectable cheeseburgers. You only have room in your stomach for one cheeseburger, so you cannot eat both. Which cheeseburger do you pick? You can arbitrarily select either cheeseburger without being irrational. This is because you have good reason to select either cheeseburger, and good reason to arbitrarily choose one. You have good reason to select either cheeseburger because both satisfy your goal of not being hungry. You have good reason to arbitrarily select one of the cheeseburgers because if you do not, you will remain hungry. The arbitrary action is nested within a context of choices that are grounded in reason. It seems to me that God can perform nested arbitrary actions if he finds himself in situations where he is presented with two or more equally good options that would satisfy his overall rational goals. In those cases, God has a good reason to perform a nested arbitrary action. What is unacceptable is God performing utterly arbitrary actions, which are actions performed for no reason whatsoever.

Second, if you deny God's perfect rationality, you diminish the perfect personhood of God and our ability to have a close personal relationship with God. Persons act for reasons. That is a unique feature about persons as compared to non-personal substances like rocks and trees. Understanding a person's reason for acting as she does is crucial for developing an intimate relationship with her, and for judging if she is a trustworthy person. When we empathize with another person, part of what that involves is coming to understand the reasons for why this other person thinks, feels, and acts as she does. From there, you can judge if this other person is a trustworthy individual with whom you can have a close relationship.

12. Lebens, *Principles of Judaism*, 75.

If you come to see that a particular individual consistently acts on a whim instead of with reason, it is difficult to be close to that person. You cannot trust wildly arbitrary people. Nor can you partner with wildly arbitrary people through promoting their interests and projects. If a person is wildly arbitrary, you cannot know what her projects and interests are because her interests and projects shift with every fleeting moment. That, in turn, makes it difficult to promote her projects and interests.

If God does not create the universe for a particular reason, it is going to be difficult for us to enter into a close relationship with God. We cannot engage in empathy to understand why God acted in the way that he did. His particular projects with creation would not have a purpose, and that makes it difficult for us to promote God's projects. Whereas, if God is perfectly rational, we can trust that there is a plan or purpose for creation. If we come to understand God's desires and motivations, we can enter into a closer relationship with God, and figure out how to promote God's projects.

To be clear, I am not saying that I understand all of God's reasons for creating a universe, nor do I know all of God's reasons for doing the many things that he does. But nothing terribly interesting follows from that. In most cases of personal relationships, we do not know nor understand all of the reasons that others have for their feelings and actions. Yet we can still develop meaningful relationships because we can come to some partial understanding of other people's reasons, desires, goals, and so on. The same is true of our relationship with God. The more we come to understand God's reasons, the closer we can be with God.

For example, say that you come to know that one of God's reasons for creating you is so that you can enter into a loving relationship with God. That would give you some insight into the kind of person that God is, and give you a reason for entering into a close relationship with God. Things are rather different if you discovered that God had no reason for creating you, and no reason for sending you to hell for all eternity, but he still created and damned you. That would give you good reason to not want a close relationship with God.

Now that I have stressed the importance of God's perfect rationality, I wish to return to the General Problem of Creation and the Particular Problem of Creation. Following the suggestion from Amyraut, answering these questions will lead to a discussion on predestination and providence.

WHY CREATE ANYTHING AT ALL?

According to Jonathan Edwards,

That which God had primarily in view in creating, and the original ordination of the world, must be constantly kept in view, and have a governing influence in all God's works, or with respect to everything he does towards his creatures.[13]

God's reason for creating in general will determine the framework for God's subsequent choices and actions. If God creates a universe in order to watch electrons spin in the void, then God's subsequent actions will be focused on achieving that goal. God will select from a range of possible universes that have electrons in them. God will not choose universes that have no electrons because that would not satisfy his particular goal. If God creates the universe in order to enter into friendship with sentient creatures, then God's subsequent choices and actions will be focused on achieving this particular goal. God will not decide to create a universe where human life is impossible. God will choose from a range of universes in which human life is actually possible, and perhaps inevitable.

It seems to me that there are many different reasons for why God would create in general. The primary reason seems to be in order to bring about certain kinds of valuable things that would not exist otherwise. What I have just said might sound obvious, but it has not been the clear answer throughout Christian history. Historically, classical theists have said that God perfectly realizes all values in himself. All of the possible goods are essentially realized in God without creation. Thus, God cannot create more good things.[14] If that is the case, then there is no reason to create a universe because God cannot add any more value to the universe.[15] I just think that this is deeply mistaken.

If God had not created anything at all, then a great many of valuable things would not exist. There is a value to having electrons spinning in a void. It might not be much value, but it is a value that would not exist if God had not created. There is a kind of beauty in the vast landscape of the universe that cosmologists are only beginning to investigate. That is a valuable thing that would not exist if God had not created. Then, of course, there is a great value to having loving Creator-creature relationships. Those valuable relationships with those valuable creatures would not exist if God had not created anything.

Anyone familiar with the history of Western philosophical theology might raise an objection at this point. A classical theist who has read far too

---

13. Schultz, *Jonathan Edwards' "Concerning the End for Which God Created the World,"* 15.

14. Murphy, *God's Own Ethics*, 80–81.

15. Ward, *Christ and the Cosmos*, 25–26.

much Plato and not enough Scripture might complain that if God somehow gains anything from creation, then God is lacking in perfection. Often times the objection will go on to say that if God gains anything of value from creation, then God needs creation.[16] In which case, God is not really self-sufficient.[17] Sometimes Christian theologians will even point to Acts 17:25 to establish that God has no needs in order to bolster this argument.

I must confess that I cannot feel the force of these kinds of objections. Every version of the objection that I am aware of contains a significant number of controversial philosophical assumptions that the Christian need not accept. To start, most versions seem to forget the basic definition of self-sufficiency. It means that God's essential perfect nature is not dependent upon anything outside of himself. Remember that God's perfect nature is all of the great-making properties. God does not lack any great-making properties, nor does God get his great-making properties from something else. I can understand why God does not lack anything in this sense. God does not lack any perfections. Yet there is another sense in which God lacks all sorts of things. If God exists all alone, then God lacks electrons spinning in the void. Does God lacking these electrons somehow undermine his perfection? I cannot see a plausible way to answer yes to that question. When God creates, he gains some electrons. Does this gain in electrons somehow add to God's perfection? Hardly! *Being the creator of electrons* is not a great-making property. When one thinks of it in this way, the negative connotations of the word *lack* seem to disappear, thus gutting the objection of its rhetorical force.

Next, consider the word *need*. In every version of the objection that I am aware of there is a wild leap to God *needing* creation. Why should I think that if God creates to bring about valuable things that God somehow needs those valuable things? As children, we learned the difference between needing something and wanting something. Sometimes I get the impression that some theologians did not learn this basic childhood lesson. God can recognize the potential value of created things, and that can give God a reason to want to create those things. After all, it would be pretty great to create a universe. But is the universe so utterly amazing that God *needs* to create it? I'm going to need to see an argument to persuade me of that. As I see it, God's reason to create is in order to bring about values that would not otherwise exist. These potential values are things that God wants, but they are not so incredibly valuable that they compel God to create.

16. Strong, *Systematic Theology*, 2:398.

17. Schultz, Jonathan Edwards' "*Concerning the End for Which God Created the World*," 49–50.

Notice something important here. If one says that God's reason to create is to bring about values that would otherwise not exist, this only answers the General Problem of Creation. In fact, it only gives us a very general answer to that problem. This is because God has a seemingly unlimited amount of options available to himself for what valuable things he could create. God could create a single angel, or a single electron. God could create a universe with nothing but shrimp, or a universe completely void of shrimp. God could create a single universe or a multiverse. God has a lot of valuable options. This does not bring us any closer to addressing the Particular Problem of Creation.

In order to get closer to addressing the Particular Problem of Creation, one will need to specify some divine reasons for creating in general that would lead to God focusing on a particular subset of valuable options. I say "subset" because I wish to avoid one particular kind of answer to the General and Particular Problem of Creation. One kind of answer to the General Problem of Creation says that divine goodness is necessarily diffusive. What this means is that God necessarily has to create as many valuable things as possible.[18] This is sometimes called the Dionysian Principle of Plenitude. On this principle, God must create all possible valuable things. Once you accept this, you have an easy answer to the Particular Problem of Creation. For any possible thing that would be valuable for God to create, God must create it. Why does this particular universe exist? Because God had to create it along with all of the other possible universes and their timelines.

The Dionysian Principle of Plenitude sounds nice at first glance because it gives you an answer to the General and Particular Problems of Creation that focuses on just how amazingly good God is. Yet the consequences for this view are pretty dire. To start, notice that God *must* create. God necessarily creates everything. God has no free will on this scenario. Sometimes theologians committed to the Principle of Plenitude will respond by saying that God's freedom is beyond the binary of necessity and contingency, so in some mysterious way God is still free even though God necessarily has no ability to do otherwise. I find such "beyond" language to be oddly convenient. It is a great card to play when one is faced with a serious objection that one cannot answer. Of course, these same theologians will not let anyone else play the "beyond" card when they are offering objections to their opponent's view. I think that this demonstrates just how intellectually bankrupt the "beyond" card really is. Playing this card does not change the fact that the Principle of Plenitude has removed God's freedom.

18. Morris, *Our Idea of God*, 146–48.

If that were not bad enough, the Principle of Plenitude can also remove creaturely freedom. If God must create all possible universes and timelines, then the entire way the world is, is the only way the entire world can be. Things could not be otherwise for God must necessarily ensure that they are exactly this way. This is called a modal collapse. A modal collapse occurs when the distinct categories of necessity and contingency are collapsed into a single category. In this case, everything is collapsed into the category of necessity.

A modal collapse strikes most theologians and philosophers as implausible. Here is why. Look at what shirt you are wearing. Could you have worn a different shirt today? Surely you could have worn a different shirt today. Or consider the electron near your left elbow. Could that electron have been just a smidge closer to your elbow? Again, the answer seems to be yes. Or consider the grace that God gave to you for your salvation. Could God have refrained from giving you grace? Again, the answer seems to be yes. Grace, by definition, is supposed to be a free gift from God that God did not have to give. Yet on a modal collapse, the answer to these questions is a resounding no.

On a modal collapse, things cannot possibly be otherwise than the way they are. You are reading this book right now. You could not possibly be doing anything else, given a modal collapse. Think of all the evil events happening around you as you read this book. Typically, theologians say that God permits or allows evil to exist for a good reason. A modal collapse prevents one from saying this. On a modal collapse, God cannot permit or allow anything. Permitting or allowing implies that God could have done otherwise, such as preventing the evil that exists. On a modal collapse, God cannot do otherwise, so any notion of permitting evaporates. Clearly, God's freedom and your freedom have evaporated. No amount of "beyond" language can convince us otherwise because on a modal collapse the scenario of us being otherwise convinced is impossible.

The modal collapse, and its eradication of divine and creaturely freedom, has led most Christian theologians and philosophers to be wary of the Principle of Plenitude. To be sure, many have flirted with the Dionysian Principle. It is hard not to flirt with it because it has an initial attractiveness. Yet hardly any theologian is willing to bite the bullet and accept the consequences of it, though there are some notable exceptions. As for myself, I have flirted with the Dionysian Principle, and decided that I am not really attracted to its pseudo-account of goodness and freedom. We had our moments, but I decided that it is best that we part ways.

As I understand things, God does not do all that he could possibly do. As I discussed in the previous chapter, God's freedom actually rules out the ability to actualize all possibilities because the very exercise of freedom entails ruling out certain possibilities. For now, I wish to follow the majority of theologians and say that God only brings about a subset of the possible valuable things that he could bring about. God's reasons for creating in general are to actualize values that would not otherwise obtain. Yet not just any old values are in view here. God may wish to actualize all sorts of kinds of values, but I believe that certain particular values are toward the top of God's list. These particular values are to create a material universe that can have some degree of autonomy that contain the kind of creatures that God can enter into loving relationships with.[19]

Again, I do not claim to know all of God's reasons for creating in general. What I am claiming is that one of God's most central purposes in creating is to enter into loving relationships with humans. According to Jordan Wessling, the gospel of John makes it clear that one of God's goals is to befriend humans.[20] Call this God's *Most Central Purpose* (MCP).[21]

> MCP: God's most central purpose for creating the universe is to enter into friendship with as many human persons as possible.

As I see it, the MCP is a natural purpose for God to have. I think that it is grounded in the loving nature of God. This decision to create a universe so that creatures can enjoy everlasting friendship with God is not based on any foreseen creaturely free action or merit. Instead, this decision is grounded in God's natural desire to have friendship with any and all self-conscious creatures that he might possibly create. This desire is a necessary entailment of God's perfect goodness or love.[22] Thus, one can say that God's decision to create is grounded in God's perfectly loving nature, and not on something external to God. Call this the Universalist Desire.

> Universalist Desire: God desires to have a genuine, everlasting friendship with any self-conscious creature that He might possibly make.

The Universalist Desire can help answer the General Problem of Creation because it identifies a general motivation for God to create a universe. Also, notice that the Universalist Desire is weaker than the Dionysian Principle of Plenitude. The Dionysian Principle says that God must necessarily create. The Universalist Desire does not necessitate that God create. It

19. Adams, *Christ and Horrors*, 39.
20. Wessling, *Love Divine*, 24.
21. Rice, *The Future of Open Theism*, 230.
22. Mawson, *Divine Attributes*, 46.

simply says that God has a desire to have friendship with any self-conscious creature that he might possibly make. God wants friendship with creatures, but he does not need it.

The Universalist Desire can also put us one step closer to addressing the Particular Problem of Creation because it will narrow down the range of universes that God might create. What kind of universe would God need to create in order to offer everlasting friendship to self-conscious creatures? A perfectly rational God will create the kind of universe that best satisfies the Universalist Desire. It certainly will not be a universe with nothing but electrons spinning in the void because a universe like that does not have self-conscious creatures that can enter into genuine friendship with God. I do not care what the panpsychist says; electrons spinning in the void are not conscious or proto-conscious beings. The Universalist Desire can only be satisfied by universes with conscious and autonomous agents.

As omniscient, God knows that there are constraints on how self-conscious creatures can enjoy everlasting friendship with God. Genuine friendship requires significant freedom on the part of God and creatures. Further, self-conscious creatures will have to be established in virtue in order to have a deep friendship with God. Nonetheless, God has the desire to have a friendship with any and all self-conscious creatures that he might make. Only certain particular universes can provide the environment where something like this can take place. (I will return to this in the next chapter.)

One can say that the Universalist Desire serves as a policy or constraint on the kinds of possible universes that God considers for creation. Desires can naturally be said to be fundamental to the divine psychology, and thus prior to any decision that God might make. For example, the Christian God naturally desires that truth, beauty, and goodness be upheld for all eternity. Thus, one can say that God's desires guide his selection of a possible universe to create.

A theologian can also emphasize a second desire in God that guides his selection of a possible universe to create. Call it the Incarnation Anyway Desire.[23]

> Incarnation Anyway Desire: God desires an incarnation because it is the best, or most fitting way, to achieve the Universalist Desire.

One can say that it is natural, or fitting, that God should desire the closest possible friendship or union with his self-conscious creatures. An

---

23. Cf. Driel, *Incarnation Anyway*. Adams, *Christ and Horrors*, 174–81. Crisp, *Analyzing Doctrine*, ch. 6.

incarnation demonstrates a deep solidarity with his self-conscious creatures no matter what kind of universe God might create. Moreover, an incarnation would demonstrate an offer of friendship that is universal in scope to all of God's self-conscious creatures.[24] Thus, the Incarnation Anyway Desire can guide God's selection of a possible universe to create. In the next chapter, I shall set up the Particular Problem of Creation, and explore potential answers in the remainder of the book.

---

24. Mawson, *Divine Attributes*, 46.

6

What Are God's Creative Options?

THE NEXT QUESTION THAT I would like to address is this: Why this particular universe instead of any other? However, I cannot answer that question without first exploring what God's options are. Things get messy here because there are different kinds of universes that God might create related to different doctrines of divine providence and foreknowledge. In this chapter I shall explore some of God's options. I'll try to address the costs and benefits of each kind of universe in this chapter and the next. Before doing that, I will paint in broad strokes. I will discuss the general features that a universe will need in order to satisfy God's desire to enter into friendship with human persons.

FRIENDSHIP WITH GOD AND THE REQUIREMENT OF HUMAN FREEDOM

God has created humans with the goal of entering into genuine friendship with them.[1] Brian Leftow offers some reflections on friendship with God, and human freedom. He starts by noting that God desires to be friends with humans in Scripture (Exod 3:11; Isa 41:8; Job 29:4). Then he asks about how God can bring about friendship. Leftow makes a fairly common claim—friendship requires freedom. He says that most friendships begin in some kind of involuntary attraction, but that people choose whether or not to continue the relationship and turn it into a genuine friendship. He writes,

---

1. Evans, *God and Moral Obligation*, 31.

> Friendship is a deliberately pursued project, for we seek our friends' company, seek to know them better, to further their interests, and to keep ourselves attractive to them. Further, we commit ourselves to our friends. Fair-weather friends aren't true friends. A true friend is someone you can count on. A true friend is committed to stand by us and help in times of trouble, and will if the time comes to choose to honor that commitment.[2]

The emphasis on freedom is important to note here. Leftow says,

> Genuine commitment cannot be coerced. Nor can the rest of friendship. We can be forced to act friendly, but we cannot be forced into genuine friendship; in fact, attempts to force us may make us cease even to like the person coercing us.[3]

If God's most central purpose in creating this universe is to enter into a genuine friendship with humans, then God cannot coerce that friendship. Coercion breeds all manner of bad emotions and beliefs that lead to broken relationships. For example, coercion can lead the coerced to feel resentment, fear, and hatred toward the one manipulating them. Any positive emotions would seem to be the result of brainwashing or Stockholm Syndrome. That is not a genuine friendship. According to Leftow, God's perfect love places constraints on how God can bring about genuine friendship with humans. He argues,

> If God gave creatures natures which guaranteed that they would love, trust and commit to Him, this would be relevantly like brainwashing or coercion. Our response would come ultimately from God, not us. God would frustrate His goal of befriending us. So God can befriend us only by giving us natures which leave us free to reject this friendship. Because God imposes our natures on us, if God genuinely wants to be friends, He must impose natures which leaves us free to reject this friendship.[4]

In light of this, one can start to think about the kind of universe that God needs to create in order to provide the opportunity for genuine divine-human friendship.

---

2. Leftow, "Perfect Being Theology and Friendship," 107.
3. Leftow, "Perfect Being Theology and Friendship," 107.
4. Leftow, "Perfect Being Theology and Friendship," 108.

THE GENERAL FEATURES OF A FRIENDLY UNIVERSE

Recall again God's *Most Central Purpose* (MCP).[5] In the previous chapter, I defined it as follows:

> MCP: God's most central purpose for creating the universe is to enter into friendship with as many human persons as possible.

If God is going to satisfy the MCP, then God must select a particular kind of universe. Not just any old universe will do. It needs to be a universe where self-conscious life is not only possible, but inevitable. This significantly narrows down the range of universes that God might create. In the previous chapter, I also discussed God's Incarnation Anyway Desire. Whatever universe God creates will need to be such that God can become incarnate within it. What kind of universe can satisfy all of that? To be honest, I don't know for sure. My guess is that lots of different kinds of universes can do all of that, but I can discuss some of the general features that a universe must have if it is going to be a potential candidate for creation. Call this range of universes *friendly universes* because they are universes with creatures that can enter into genuine friendship with God. My guess is that the range of friendly universes is quite large, though not as large as the range of all possible universes. In this section, I will discuss some of the general features of the friendly universes.

To start, a general feature of a friendly universe is that it contain creatures that can possibly enter into friendship with God. These kinds of creatures are persons. Keeping in mind the MCP, William Hasker says that it is good that there should be free, rational, and responsible persons. It is good that persons should have occasion and opportunity to exercise their inherent powers and potentialities in order to develop an individual character. Hasker also says that it is good that persons be joined together into families and communities in which persons are responsible to and for each other. This allows for more opportunities for created persons to develop their individual character in greater and morally significant ways. Finally, Hasker says that it is good that the structures and processes of human societies develop from within, utilizing the powers, potential, and ingenuity of the members of those societies, rather than those structures being imposed on society by God.[6]

What kind of universe would God need to create in order for these goods to be possible? Hasker says that we should expect God to create a particular kind of universe with stable laws of nature that allow for a variety

---

5. Rice, *Future of Open Theism*, 230.
6. Hasker, "Open Theist View," 71–73.

of creatures with varying degrees of complexity, flexibility, and autonomy. The complexity of creatures ranges from simple atoms to rational animals. The kind of autonomy in view here is the freedom of an entity to operate according to its inherent capabilities without direct control or interference from God. According to Hasker, it is a great good that God should create a universe with component systems that are able to evolve from within by utilizing its inherent powers and potentialities.[7] This is the kind of natural universe that one would expect God to create in order to satisfy various divine purposes in general, but also the MCP. This is because this is the kind of natural universe needed in order to make it possible for created persons with significant freedom to exist.

Whatever else a friendly universe might include, it needs to be a universe with stable laws of nature that allow for complexity and autonomy. This is a universe in which God will fully determine the initial conditions of the universe so as to endow it with certain powers and structure that will give rise to the kind of values or goods that he wants from creation.[8] This fully determinate set of initial conditions grounds the possible timelines that can subsequently follow.

Branching from God's precreation moment are all possible timelines. When God decides to create a universe, many possible timelines become no longer possible. When God fully determines the set of initial conditions for the universe, even more possible timelines are eliminated from being realized. Yet there are still a great many possible futures branching from this initial creative act. Some of these possible futures are good timelines and some are dark timelines. A good timeline is a possible future in which the MCP is realized. A dark timeline is a possible future in which the MCP fails to be realized. Given that God is perfectly good and rational, God will seek to eliminate dark timelines from possibly becoming actual.

God can eliminate certain dark timelines by selecting good initial conditions for the universe. For example, there is the much discussed fine-tuning of the universe.[9] These discussions reveal that there are many ways for the universe to go wrong in the moments shortly after the big bang. On some scenarios, the universe could have collapsed in on itself, thus making biological life impossible. On other scenarios, the universe could have expanded at the wrong rate, again making biological life impossible. If biological life became impossible shortly after the big bang, then the MCP would

---

7. Hasker, "Open Theist View," 63–66.
8. Hasker, "Adequate God," 219.
9. Collins, "Teleological Argument."

fail to be realized. Thus, God selected favorable initial conditions that would prevent these dark timelines from occurring.

As Hasker and others point out, a universe with natural laws and created persons with freedom involves various risks. Stable natural laws bring with them the risk of natural disasters occurring. Creatures with significant moral freedom bring with them the risk of immoral actions. Discussion of these matters is commonplace in theology and philosophy of religion, though the details of the actual biological laws needed to pull this off are scarce. Emanuela Sani and I have elsewhere discussed the potential for God to use redundancies, risk-management, and surveillance systems in the biological order to lower various risks, and in order to guarantee the MCP. Thus giving the details of the kind of the biological laws that one should expect God to put in place.[10] In order to keep this relatively short, I shall ask interested readers to check out the details of biological order there. Here, I shall focus on other features of a friendly universe.

If one of God's goals is to create human persons who can enter into a genuine friendship with him, then God will need to ensure that humans have a certain set of cognitive equipment that is primed for friendship. I have already stated that freedom is essential to friendship. Yet, there are certain other cognitive powers that are needed in order to make possible genuine relationships between God and humans to ensure that dark timelines are eliminated. A standard package of cognitive mechanisms will also include the powers of rationality, emotion, empathy, and a theory of mind.

I start with the theory of mind, which is the ability to recognize other minds. The theory of mind has been much discussed in the literature on psychology and philosophy of religion.[11] Alvin Plantinga has famously extended the theory of mind to a faculty for an innate awareness of God called the *sensus divinitatis*.[12] Endowing humans with such a faculty would help eliminate dark timelines because without this faculty, humans would be unable to be aware of God.

Yet simply recognizing other minds, like God, would not be enough to ensure the success of the MCP. Humans endowed with the ability to recognize other minds and perform free actions is not sufficient for accepting God's offer of friendship. In order to enter into genuine relationships, creatures will need to have the cognitive powers of rationality and emotion. These cognitive powers are said to enable people to share ideas, take

10. Mullins and Sani, "Open Theism and Risk Management."

11. Visala, "Human Cognition and the Image of God," 104–5.

12. Plantinga, *Warranted Christian Belief*. For an introductory debate over this cognitive mechanism within evolutionary psychology, see Bulbulia, "Bayes and the Evolution of Religious Beliefs," and Murray and Schloss, "Evolutionary Accounts of Religion."

responsibility for their actions, and develop trust and cooperation.[13] All of which are important for friendship.

Rationality and emotion go hand-in-hand.[14] The power of rationality is the ability to be responsive to reasons for acting.[15] There are different kinds of roles that reasons play in our free actions such as justifying, motivating, and explaining the actions of an agent.[16] Often, reasons for acting are values or disvalues in a given situation. Emotions play a crucial role in helping agents identify reasons for action because emotions involve evaluations.[17] As I have said before, emotions are felt evaluations of situations that involve perceiving various values or disvalues in a given circumstance.[18] When one has an emotion, one is perceiving the value of the object of her emotion to be an object that is worthy of her attention and worthy of her action.[19] Thus, there is a close connection between the emotional evaluations and acting for a reason. If an emotional response fails to properly track the value of the object, the emotional response is not rational. If an emotional response properly tracks the value of the object, the emotional response is rational.[20]

God endowing humans with these cognitive powers is a great example of a risk-management system built into the psychology of human nature. God is the supreme object of value. By endowing humans with the cognitive powers of reason and emotion, God has enabled humans to be capable of recognizing God's value and appropriately respond to God's value. Thus, enabling humans to accept God's offer of friendship. If humans lacked these cognitive powers, they would be unable to accept God's offer of friendship, and the MCP would fail.

Along with a theory of mind, rationality, and emotion, humans will need the capacity for empathy in order to enter into friendship with God. The capacity for empathy is a person's ability to understand what it is like for another person to feel the way that they do. In empathizing with others, a person comes to know what others care about and their reasons for acting as they do. Empathy plays a large role in the development of genuine

---

13. Visala, "Human Cognition and the Image of God," 104.
14. Cf. Clore, "Psychology and the Rationality of Emotion."
15. Pearson, *Rationality, Time, and Self*, 122.
16. Pearson, *Rationality, Time, and Self*, 68.
17. Cf. Brady, *Emotional Insight*.
18. Roberts, *Emotions in the Moral Life*, 114–15. Todd, "Emotion and Value," 706.
19. Helm, "Augustinian-Calvinist View," 195.
20. Todd, "Emotion and Value," 704.

relationships.[21] This is so for at least two reasons. First, individuals with a reduced capacity for empathy also have a reduced capacity to form attachments to others.[22] The higher the capacity for empathy, the higher the capacity to form attachments and genuine friendship. Second, human persons naturally want to be understood because there is a kind of loneliness that comes when others cannot understand why you are feeling as you do. This is because humans do not bond with people who do not understand them, whereas humans do bond with people who do empathetically understand them.[23] The natural human desire to be understood can draw creatures to seek out the maximally empathetic God.[24] By endowing human persons with these cognitive powers, God has ensured that humans are primed to genuinely accept his offer of friendship. Thus, God is able to eliminate a large number of dark timelines in which the MCP fails.

Earlier I mentioned that there are certain risks in creating a natural world with free creatures. Many philosophers argue that creating a universe like this is necessary in order to make the MCP possible. A common claim is that if God wants humans to be in a genuine relationship with him, then humans must have a particular kind of virtuous character. Good friendships are based on shared interests and mutual trust. If God desires to have friendship with humans, then God desires that humans be trustworthy.[25] The question becomes what kind of universe is required for humans to develop the requisite moral character for friendship with God. I wish to point out two further features of a friendly universe: epistemic distance and the possibility for suffering.

I will start with epistemic distance. Epistemic distance basically means that some particular item of knowledge is not immediately and overwhelmingly obvious. The case of interest here is the existence and nature of God. God cannot make his own existence and presence overwhelmingly obvious. Why? If humans were immediately aware of the full presence of God, they would never freely develop their moral character.[26] Think about it like this:

When I was fifteen, I went to a Christian youth convention. For whatever reason that year, the speakers had decided on a certain set of slogans to repeat over and over. One slogan went something like, "Don't do anything that you would not do if Jesus Christ were in the room with you." If

21. Cf. Betzler, "Relational Value of Empathy."
22. Brito et al., "Psychopathy," 1–3.
23. Morton, "Empathy and Imagination," 183–84.
24. McConnell, *Christlike God*, 121–22.
25. Holtzen, "Friends with Benefits," 95–96.
26. Hick, "Irenaen Theodicy," 43. Cf. Swinburne, *Existence of God*, 269.

I remember correctly, this slogan had the goal of persuading teenagers to avoid pornography. I have no idea if this slogan helped. For me, my mind immediately went elsewhere. I started thinking of all the things that I would not do if Jesus walked into the room. For some reason my first thought was that I would not watch TV. Something seemed impolite about watching TV when a guest has just arrived. Especially when that guest is Jesus Christ. Then I started thinking about other cases. At some point I will need to go to the bathroom. I would not feel comfortable doing that with Jesus standing there. Then, being fifteen, I started thinking about when I am married. There are certain morally permissible things to do on my wedding night, and I most certainly would not do any of that with Jesus standing there. In my fifteen-year-old mind I decided that this slogan could not be a good moral principle to live by. As an adult, I still think that is correct.

If humans are born with an immediate and innate awareness of the full presence of God, they will not be able to freely develop into the kind of virtuous beings that God wants them to be. Notice that this is not inconsistent with God implanting in humans a *sensus divinitatis*. The claim that I am making is that there needs to be some epistemic distance between God and humans such that humans are not immediately and perpetually aware of the full presence of God. Leftow says that God cannot overwhelmingly bias our nature toward friendship. If my response to God is 95 percent implanted in me by God, then I am 95 percent brainwashed by God.[27] God can implant in us the *sensus divinitatis* and provide evidence of his existence and nature in all manner of ways, but God must be careful not to coerce our friendship with him. As Leftow explains,

> Thus God has a tightrope to walk. The more God biases our natures toward Him, the less genuine our friendship. Yet if God were to bias our natures against friendship, the less likely our friendship would be.[28]

Leftow claims that God must find an optimum balance where God does not overwhelm us and coerce friendship. He says that he does not know what that optimum balance is, and I make no claims to know either. Leftow suggests that whatever that balance is, it probably is a slight bias toward friendship with God, but not too much. A slight balance toward God leaves it as "robustly possible" that large numbers of people will reject God's offer of friendship. He says, "Because of what friendship is and God's

---

27. Leftow, "Perfect Being Theology and Friendship," 109.
28. Leftow, "Perfect Being Theology and Friendship," 109.

position as our creator, if God seeks our friendship, we should expect Him to endure a good deal of rejection, which is of course what we see."[29]

So one feature of a friendly universe is epistemic distance. The final feature of a friendly universe that I wish to talk about is the possibility of suffering. I should note an irony here in calling such a universe a *friendly* universe. Again, a friendly universe is one in which genuine friendship with God is possible. It does sound strange to say that a friendly universe must include the possibility of suffering, and yet here we are. A common claim from theologians and philosophers is that God must place creatures in an environment where they can genuinely develop their moral character through a long series of significantly weighty moral choices.[30] This involves an environment where there is the real possibility of harm, pain, and suffering.

A famous example of this line of thought comes from John Hick's so-called soul-building theodicy. For Hick, God must create a universe with real consequences for human actions. Otherwise, humans cannot develop a moral character. Hick writes,

> A world in which there can be no pain or suffering would also be one in which there can be no moral choices and hence no possibility of moral growth and development. For in a situation in which no one can ever suffer injury or be liable to pain or suffering there would be no distinction between right and wrong action. No action would be morally wrong, because no action could have harmful consequences; and likewise no action would be morally right in contrast to wrong. Whatever values of such a world, it clearly could not serve a purpose of the development of its inhabitants from self-regarding animality to self-giving love.[31]

Both Hick and Richard Swinburne argue that a universe with the possibility of real harm is required in order to bring about the great goods of soul-making and friendship with God. The possibility of suffering makes possible greater goods like genuine freedom and moral development, sympathy and compassion, and more.[32] The actual development of human moral character into virtuous people is a prerequisite for a deep and abiding friendship with God. So as odd as it sounds, a general feature of a friendly universe is that it include the possibility of suffering.

29. Leftow, "Perfect Being Theology and Friendship," 109–110.
30. Hick, "Irenaen Theodicy," 44.
31. Hick, "Irenaen Theodicy," 47–48.
32. Hick, *Evil and the Love of God*, 334–35. Swinburne, *Existence of God*, 257–58.

I take these to be the general features of friendly universes. I assume that there are other features of friendly universes that I have missed, and I know of other features that I am ignoring for the sake of brevity. I ask others to think about this issue more deeply. Perhaps one day we can come up with a more detailed account together.

Before moving forward, it is worth noticing that this discussion of friendly universes does not exactly answer the Particular Problem of Creation. It puts us one step closer to answering the Particular Problem of Creation, but it does not give us a full answer. In what follows, I wish to consider some possible starting points for fuller answers to the Particular Problem of Creation.

THE DIFFERENT KINDS OF UNIVERSES

In order to keep the discussion short and relatively readable, I will narrow down to consider three kinds of friendly universes that God might create related to the three dominant theories of providence. I will call these Calvinist universes, Molinist universes, and open universes. In this section, I will briefly describe these kinds of universes. In the next section, I will explain how each can seemingly help answer the Problem of God's Unfulfilled Desires.

Calvinist and Molinist universes share something in common that open universes do not have. Calvinist and Molinist universes come with a specific timeline. For each Calvinist and Molinist universe, there is an associated timeline that describes exactly how the future will unfold. This is not true of open universes. Each open universe comes with a wide array of possible futures. Which possible future timeline will come about is an open question. With that being said, I want to get into some of the specifics, starting with Calvinist universes.

Those who affirm some version of theological determinism claim that God knows the future because God causally determines everything that will happen. Not all theological determinists are Calvinists, of course, but the label of Calvinism is a good enough shorthand for my purposes here. Call Calvinist universes any universe in which God freely decides to causally determine everything that shall take place in the timeline. Many people have worries about how humans can have free will if God causes them to act as they do. I have very similar worries, but I will set those aside. Some theological determinists maintain that human freedom is compatible with being causally determined by God. Those are the views that I am interested in at the moment. They have many clever ways to explain how human freedom is compatible with divine determinism, and I will not be questioning those here.[33] For this conversation, I will grant that compatibilism about free will and divine determinism is coherent. Instead, I will consider some other kinds of objections to it in the next chapter.

A Molinist universe is one in which God is said to employ his middle knowledge in order to establish a universe and specific timeline with creatures who are not fully determined by God to perform their actions. These creatures are said to have libertarian freedom—freedom that is not compatible with being causally determined by God. As with determinism, Molinism faces various objections. Some complain that Molinism is really just theological determinism in disguise. Others complain that middle knowledge is incoherent. Those are important objections, but I have nothing terribly interesting to say about them here. Instead, I shall consider some problems for Molinism in the next chapter.

An open universe is one in which God does not know exactly how the future will unfold. God has given creatures libertarian freedom, and because of this, God cannot know exactly how things will turn out. People who affirm this view are called open theists. Sometimes open theists talk about God taking a risk when he creates an open universe.[34] Since God does not know exactly how the future will unfold, it might seem that the MCP could fail. However, Sani and I have argued that open theists have exaggerated the amount of risk that God takes.[35] On open theism, God is said to have developed an exhaustive contingency plan prior to creation. As I see it, this exhaustive contingency plan includes preventing all potential dark timelines from becoming actual. God has figured out all of the potential ways to bring about the MCP, and it is guaranteed that he will not rest until he in fact brings about the MCP.

THE PROBLEM OF GOD'S UNFULFILLED DESIRES

One will recall from earlier the Problem of God's Unfulfilled Desires. To remind you of the problem, it looks like this. God is said to desire the salvation of everyone, but not everyone accepts God's offer of friendship. Of course, that is assuming that universalism is false. If you are a universalist, then you won't be bothered by this problem.

---

33. Furlong, *Challenges of Divine Determinism*.
34. Sanders, *God Who Risks*.
35. Mullins and Sani, "Open Theism and Risk Management." Mullins, "Divine Temporality and Providential Bodgery."

Here is a traditional way of stating the question: how could God decree that all be saved, but some fail to accept God's offer of friendship? After all, the efficacy of God's decrees are infallible. What God has decreed must come to pass. This problem has lead various Reformed theologians to deny unlimited atonement and instead affirm that Christ's offer of salvation only extends to those whom God elected prior to creation.

I think that limited atonement is unbiblical. Instead I think that God's offer of friendship and salvation is universal in scope. In what follows, I will try to offer a way for theological determinists (e.g., Calvinists), Molinists, and open theists to address the Problem of God's Unfulfilled Desires.

To address this problem, start with the MCP, the Universalist Desire, and the Incarnation Anyway Desire. With these 2 desires in place, one can give an account of God's hypothetical universalism. Unlike decrees, desires can go unfulfilled without any obvious loss to divine sovereignty.[36] A decree determines that certain outcomes will obtain. Decrees are not the sort of things that can go unfulfilled. A desire, however, is merely wanting the world to be a certain way in the future. A divine desire can go unfulfilled. To be sure, some Calvinist theologians will not like the notion of divine desires going unfulfilled, but the Calvinist cannot consistently offer a complaint here. This is because Calvinists often talk about God's desire that humans not sin, and yet also claim that God permits humans to sin.[37] Calvinists, and other determinists like Thomists, typically distinguish between God's antecedent will and consequent will, or God's moral will and his permissive will. These distinctions are meant to capture the claim that God desires that all be saved and not sin, but for some good reason God allows sin and reprobation. If this is not a problem for divine sovereignty on Calvinism, then it ought not be a problem for the Molinist or open theist either.

At the precreation moment, God surveys all of the possible universes that he might create. God's desire is to create a universe where all creatures freely enter into a deep friendship with him. However, a Christian theologian might stipulate that there are no such possible universes due to something called transworld depravity. According to Alvin Plantinga, a person has transworld depravity if there is no possible universe in which she exists and does not sin. As Plantinga points out, it is possible that every created person suffers from transworld depravity. In which case, it would be metaphysically impossible for God to create a universe with free creatures who do not sin.[38] A model of God can appeal to this in order to explain why

---

36. Vicens and Kittle, *God and Human Freedom*, 52.
37. Feinberg, *No One Like Him*, 694–98.
38. Plantinga, *Nature of Necessity*, 184–89.

God's Universalist Desire is unfulfilled. It is metaphysically impossible for God's Universalist Desire to be fulfilled, so no strike against God's sovereignty since sovereignty and omnipotence do not involve God having the ability to perform metaphysically impossible actions.[39] Since God's Universalist Desire cannot help God select which universe to create, God will need to turn to other considerations.

A theologian can say that God desires to create a universe where creatures with freedom genuinely accept God's offer of friendship. Yet God knows that the only kinds of universes and timelines where this occurs are ones in which God also offers sufficient grace. Sufficient grace is offered to everyone, but it is only efficient for some. As noted before by Louis Berkhof, efficient grace is irresistible, but it does not overpower the human person. The degree of sufficient grace given to a human person must be such that it does not coerce or manipulate the individual into accepting God's offer of friendship. Otherwise, the sufficient grace does not count as efficient grace. Instead, it becomes manipulative grace, and as stated before, most Christians don't want to affirm manipulative grace. As the Calvinist Paul Helm points out, "Some of God's actions are resistible and are resisted."[40]

Upon taking sufficient grace into consideration, the subset of possible universes and timelines shrinks considerably. God now has a smaller range to select from. Call this subset *sufficient grace universes*. On this view, there are no sufficient grace universes and timelines in which all human persons freely accept the offer of divine friendship. Why is that? Perhaps one can say that some individuals in these universes and timelines would need more grace in order to accept God's offer of friendship. Yet, the kind of grace needed would pass the threshold of efficient grace, and breach into the territory of manipulative grace. These individuals would need to be overpowered in order to accept God's offer of friendship. That kind of overpowering is not something that most theologians wish to accept.[41] Most will say that it is morally impermissible for God to engage in manipulative grace, thus further explaining why actual universalism is not possible for God to establish.

These sufficient grace universes have several features. First, they all contain an incarnation because God has the Incarnation Anyway Desire. Second, these sufficient grace universes have fallen creatures because of

---

39. I anticipate that a universalist will push back on this point. She might say that it seems quite odd that God has a desire that cannot possibly be satisfied. At this time, I have nothing to say in response, and invite universalists to develop this intuition into a full-blown argument.

40. Helm, "Augustinian-Calvinist View," 171.

41. There are notable exceptions, like the universalist Adams, *Horrendous Evils and the Goodness of God*.

transworld depravity. Third, these sufficient grace universes contain timelines with a limited number of grace infused creatures who accept God's offer of friendship, and a limited number of reprobate creatures who do not accept God's offer of friendship. Again, these creatures are reprobate because they would need to be overpowered in order to accept God's offer of friendship, and it is morally impermissible for God to engage in that kind of manipulative grace.

At this point, one might worry that this story looks too much like Molinism or open theism for any self-respecting Calvinist to accept.[42] The Molinist and open theist will be happy with this, but I think the Calvinist has nothing to worry about here either. It should be recalled that the redeemed in these possible universes are not elected because of their own merit or good faith. They are not even elected until God decrees that a particular universe and timeline should exist. The redeemed are individuals in possible universes with sufficient grace. It is God's sufficient grace that causally enables the redeemed to cooperate with the Holy Spirit, and accept God's offer of friendship. Their cooperation depends upon God's sufficient grace.

With this in mind, one can say that God has a set of possible sufficient grace universes and timelines from which to create. If one affirms meticulous providence, God's decree refers to God's selection of one of those possible universes and timelines. God's decree determines with certainty that everything that happens in that universe will in fact come to pass. Thus, God's decree is infallible, and will succeed. If one affirms a general providence, God's decree refers to his general-policies that God adopts for the purpose of satisfying the Universalist Desire to the extent which it is morally permissible and metaphysically possible for God to do so. On open theism, this decree will not specify a particular timeline, but it will include an exhaustive contingency plan to ensure that God gets the result that he wants.

With this general outline, the Calvinist, Molinist, and open theist have the basis for addressing the Problem of God's Unfulfilled Desires. With regards to the General Problem of Creation, we have an answer that appeals to God's natural and loving desires. These divine desires have not answered the Particular Problem of Creation, but they have significantly narrowed down the range of possible universes. Thus, putting us one step closer to addressing the Particular Problem of Creation.

---

42. Amyraut, *Amyraut on Predestination*, 20.

7

Why Create Any Particular Universe?

IN THE LAST CHAPTER, I identified some general features of a friendly universe. Then I discussed some possible kinds of universes that God might create. These are Calvinist, Molinist, and open universes. In this chapter, I want to look at reasons God might have for creating any particular universe. This is getting into territory where I lose my confidence and find myself uncertain what to think. I honestly don't know which particular kind of universe God has created. In this chapter I will offer reasons for and against each particular kind of universe. Part of the process of writing this out is to help me make up my own mind on the situation. Hopefully reading this will help you come one step closer to making up your own mind as well.

WHY CREATE A CALVINIST UNIVERSE?

In contemporary theology, theological determinists and open theists agree that God cannot foreknow exactly what creatures with libertarian freedom will in fact do.[1] The determinist claims that this is a point in favor of God creating a Calvinist universe. The idea is this: First, Molinism is impossible, so Molinist universes cannot be considered. This leaves God with the options of Calvinist and open universes in order to complete the MCP. In light of this, here are some alleged reasons for God to create a Calvinist universe.

---

1. Shedd, *Dogmatic Theology*, 394. Cf. Pereboom, "Libertarianism and Theological Determinism," 114. Rice, *Future of Open Theism*, 129.

Risk-Free Sovereignty. Open theists are usually pretty up front that God takes various risks when creating an open universe.[2] One such risk is allegedly the risk of failing to realize the MCP. As I have said before, I think open theists have greatly exaggerated the amount of risk involved in creating an open universe. However, for the moment, grant that there is a real risk that God could fail to bring about the MCP in an open universe. Calvinists have been quick to criticize this point, and say that a risk like that is unacceptable for God to take. With a Calvinist universe, God gets all the providential control one could possibly want. God will certainly accomplish his specific purposes for creation without any risk of divine failure.[3]

The Calvinist can say that this is a significant value in itself. The ability to realize the MCP without any risk of failure is certainly a reason in favor of creating a Calvinist universe. Yet the Calvinist can say that there are additional values at play related to friendship with God. Part of a healthy relationship is mutual trust. The Calvinist can say that risk-free sovereignty should elicit a great deal of trust from humans. If you know that God is guaranteed to bring about the MCP, that should bring you comfort that all will be well in the end.

In response to this, I think that these are values that God would consider. The ability to realize the MCP without any risk of divine failure is a value. So is the trust in God that this should bring. However, I am hesitant to say that this is a unique value for Calvinist universes. If Molinism is coherent, then Molinist universes would have both of these values too. Also, again, I think that open theists have in fact exaggerated the amount of risk that God takes when creating an open universe. For example, the open theist Gregory Boyd says that God can guarantee the success of the MCP before he creates a universe, and that this should provide assurance to humans that all will be well in the end.[4] If Boyd's position is coherent, and I think it is, then an open universe would also have these values. So there is no clear reason for God to prefer a Calvinist universe in this regard.

More Divine Knowledge. Some philosophers argue that God would have more knowledge if he created a Calvinist universe than he would if he created an open universe.[5] I'm aware of at least two ways to develop this argument. The first way goes something like this. God is omniscient. If God

2. Sanders, *God Who Risks.*
3. For a full defense of this, see Helm, *Providence of God.*
4. Boyd, "Open Future, Free Will and Divine Assurance."
5. Though Benjamin Arbour is not a Calvinist, he seems to suggest some arguments in, "A Few Worries About the Systematic Metaphysics of Open Future Open Theism." For more on his detailed account of omniscience, see Arbour, "Maximal Greatness and Perfect Knowledge."

created an open universe, God would not know the future. In which case, God is not omniscient.

This is not a good version of the argument. As I have explained before, God would still be omniscient. God is omniscient in that God knows all of the facts about reality. Prior to God's decision to create anything at all, the Calvinist says that God does not know if he will create. Is God omniscient in that state of affairs? Yes. God knows all of the facts about reality. Reality just does not include any facts about what God will in fact do at this point. Once God decides to create, God will continue to know all of the facts about reality. It is just that the facts of reality change. Once God decides to create, there are new facts; facts that God has decided to create in general, and facts about what kind of universe God has created. If God decides to create a Calvinist universe, then God will know all of the facts about reality. If God decides to create an open universe, then God will know all of the facts about reality. The only difference is that each universe includes a different set of facts for God to know. God is omniscient either way, so this argument is a failure.

Here is another way to develop the argument. If God creates a Calvinist universe, then God will know more than he would if he creates an open universe. More knowledge is a valuable thing for God to have. This provides God with a reason to create a Calvinist universe instead of an open universe.

I think that this argument is significantly better. It does seem to me that more divine knowledge is a value worth considering. Of course, this only gives the Calvinist an advantage over open theism. A Molinist can use the same argument against open theism. It does not seem obvious to me that a Molinist or a Calvinist can use this particular argument against each other. Instead, they would each have to argue that the other position is incoherent, and cannot provide the values it claims to offer.

Unfulfilled Desires. In a previous chapter, I outlined how Calvinists, Molinists, and open theists can account for God's unfulfilled desires. I relied on certain claims about transworld depravity that were developed by Molinist-friendly philosophers like Alvin Plantinga. For Molinists and open theists, it seems quite easy to account for God's unfulfilled desires. But one might doubt that Calvinism can actually address the Problem of God's Unfulfilled Desires. How could God have unfulfilled desires with all that deterministic sovereignty? Perhaps it just does not make any sense for God to have unfulfilled desires given the truth of theological determinism.

The theological determinist Derk Pereboom offers an interesting discussion on the matter. For Pereboom, a good relationship with God involves both God and humans valuing the relationship for its own sake, and both God and humans wanting what is best for each other. Throughout

Pereboom's discussion, he continually emphasizes the importance of trust for a good relationship between God and humans. Humans must be able to place their trust in God for the relationship to be good. Yet Pereboom thinks that there are several important things to consider about one's overall theological system. He says that a good relationship with God requires libertarianism if you also believe in divine retribution and eternal damnation. Things are different if you affirm universal salvation. If you affirm universal salvation, then theological determinism can accommodate a good relationship with God.[6]

This is a provocative thesis worth exploring. In this book, I am leaving open the possibility that some people will never accept God's offer of friendship.[7] This is what leads to the Problem of God's Unfulfilled Desires. If one accepts Pereboom's thesis, then one will be rejecting the notion that God does have unfulfilled desires. In other words, if universal salvation is true, then God does not have any unfulfilled desires related to his purpose of establishing genuine friendship with all human persons. I am guessing that universal salvation is not going to be acceptable to some readers, so I will stick with the assumption that it is false. If you are attracted to universalism, then what I am about to say will just give you more reasons to be a universalist.

How does Pereboom justify his thesis? He starts with some standard claims from theological determinists. The two he is concerned with here are unconditional election to eternal damnation, and retributive punishment. I will start with unconditional election. Calvinists say that prior to creation, God has decreed who will be saved and who will be damned. God's decision of who will be elected to salvation or damnation is said to be unconditional. This means that God's decision is not conditioned, or based upon, anything about the creature. Consider a creature named Damned Daniel. As you might guess, Damned Daniel has been elected for eternal damnation. Why did God decree the eternal damnation of Damned Daniel? The Calvinist says that God's decision is not based on anything about Daniel's character or actions. Nothing whatsoever about Damned Daniel factors into God's decision. That is unconditional election.

Next consider a standard account of divine retribution. Why are people being punished in hell? The Calvinist typically says that people are punished in hell because they deserve it. Something about their moral character and action entails that they deserve to be punished by God.

6. Pereboom, "Theological Determinism and the Relationship with God," 202.

7. To be sure, there are powerful arguments for universal salvation. Kronen and Reitan, *God's Final Victory*. However, I find myself with doubts about universalism. See my essay Mullins, "Philosophy of Eternal Life."

Pereboom says that unconditional election to damnation and divine retribution are inconsistent with God's goodness and love, and undermine any trust that one could have in God. Without trust, there can be no good relationship between God and humans. To see this, Pereboom offers a few reflections. First, with unconditional election it seems like God is just playing favorites, and damning people independent of any human response. Pereboom says that is not consistent with perfect goodness and love.[8] Second, this does not square with divine retribution. Given unconditional election, God did not send people to hell because of anything that they did. It is difficult to say that the damned in hell deserve punishment when the reason they are there has nothing to do with their moral character or actions. It becomes even more difficult to coherently maintain a sense of divine retribution when one recalls that this view says that God causally determines Daniel's sinful actions. What kind of God is this? This is a God who predetermines that Daniel will go to hell based on nothing about Daniel. This is a God who causally determines Daniel's sinful actions. This is a God who tells Daniel that he deserves to be punished for those divinely determined sinful actions. It is becoming increasingly difficult to describe this as a loving and just God.

I say that this is also inconsistent with God's perfect rationality. God seems to have no reason to eternally damn Daniel. At least no obvious reason like Daniel's moral character and actions. All of the obvious reasons are ruled out by unconditional election. One might say that God has a hidden reason for damning Daniel. Whatever that reason is, it will have nothing to do with Daniel's moral character and action. Perhaps the Calvinist will say that God's reason is self-revelation, but what kind of self-revelation is that? Is God the kind of being who sends people to hell for no other reason than to make his wrath known? That is a terrifying thought.

Pereboom says that this should lead one to suspect that God has a demonic disposition. Something about God's nature and decision-making in unconditional election seems inherently wicked. If you think that God is somewhat demonic, that is going to have a profoundly negative impact on your relationship with God. You certainly will not be able to trust such a being, though you will have good reason to fear God.[9] As Pereboom puts it,

> The thought that some of us might be passed over for either an unknown reason or to facilitate divine self-revelation also threatens to undermine a good relationship with God, since such a disposition would seem inconsistent with the idea that

---

8. Pereboom, "Theological Determinism and the Relationship with God," 204.
9. Pereboom, "Theological Determinism and the Relationship with God," 204–6.

God genuinely loves all of us. There are some that God could effortlessly save but doesn't. And here, again, fear and a sense of arbitrary unfairness threatens to compete with love and trust.[10]

This, and other reasons, leads Pereboom to say that the theological determinist should accept universal salvation. I will leave it up to you, my dear reader, to decide what you think about the matter.

WHY CREATE AN OPEN UNIVERSE?

Surprise! I begin with some common claims from open theists about why God would create an open universe. One common claim is that an open universe allows for the realization of certain goods that could not obtain in a Calvinist or Molinist universe. For example, an open universe provides the opportunity for divine experiences that God would not otherwise have. Richard Rice says, "With an open future, God is capable of surprise, delight, the momentary appreciation of the creatures' experiences as they happen in all their concrete detail."[11]

I don't find this claim particularly convincing. Consider a Calvinist and Molinist who affirm divine temporality and passibility.[12] Each view can say that God delights in what he has created. There is something satisfying about creating a universe, sustaining it in existence, and successfully guiding it toward the completion of God's purposes. Further, given divine empathy, God can have an appreciation for any given creature's experiences at any given moment. I fail to see how open theism owns the market on these values.

But what about divine surprise? If God creates an open universe, God does not know exactly how the future will unfold. According to Rice, this introduces an element of surprise in God's life as he creatively interacts with his creatures. I don't think that open theists see this as a knock-down reason for God to create an open universe. It is merely one kind of value that God cannot bring about if God creates a Calvinist or Molinist universe.

I do consider the element of surprise to be valuable in certain circumstances, but I am uncertain how much an open theist can push this particular value. As I have stated several times before, the Calvinist, Molinist, and open theist all agree that God does not know what he will do prior to his decision to create in general. At the so-called moment of natural knowledge,

---

10. Pereboom, "Theological Determinism and the Relationship with God," 207.
11. Rice, *Future of Open Theism*, 134.
12. E.g., Feinberg, *No One Like Him*.

God has not decided if he will create in general, and thus does not know if he will create nor what kind of universe he will create. It seems to me that a Calvinist and a Molinist could claim that they already have an element of surprise in the divine life since God does not know what he will do yet. Of course, the open theist can complain that this is not a very significant surprise. Not knowing what you will do with regards to one or two choices is not terribly exciting. Certainly nothing as exciting as the element of surprise in creating an open universe where the surprise includes a large number of creaturely activities over the course of billions of years.

I think this response from the open theist does identify a particular kind of value. The excitement of many surprises is a particular kind of value that an open universe seems to have. Yet I doubt how much this value is actually realized in an open universe. On open theism, God is said to have incredible predictive power as to what might happen. According to John Sanders, "God knows all that can possibly happen at any one time, and through his foresight and wisdom God is never caught off-guard."[13] God knows all of the possible futures, and knows the objective probability of each future obtaining. With knowledge like that, I start to lose my grasp on how surprised God can actually be.[14] Especially when I consider the fact that humans are often very predictable. We are so predictable that organizations like Cambridge Analytica can develop highly targeted advertisements to different populations, figure out how to manipulate voters, and more.

Consider a more concrete example of this. Leading up to the American civil war, various revivalist prophets started predicting that a civil war will take place. When the war started, these same prophets claimed that this was a confirmation that they were in fact prophets. The critics within the revivalist movements disagreed. They said that no amount of divine power was needed to see that the civil war was coming. The war was inevitable for anyone who knew how to read a newspaper.

If humans can make those kind of accurate predictions, then surely God's predictive power is even greater. As various events quickly approach, the objective probability about which set of actions humans will perform starts to become more and more obvious. At some point, I think it is plausible that God can know for certain which action you will perform. At the very least, God will know that it is 99 percent likely that you will perform a particular action, and God has already decided in advance how he will respond to whatever you happen to do. That does not sound like a great surprise for God. I just imagine God saying, "Ah, yes Johnny. I see what

---

13. Sanders, *God Who Risks*, 15.
14. Lukasiewicz, "On William Hasker's Theodicy," 162.

you did there. You really had me on the edge of my seat there for a bit. For a while there was only a 56 percent chance that you would make that move. But eventually, I only knew that there was a 99 percent chance that you would do that. Look at how surprised I am that you did in fact do that thing that was so overwhelmingly likely to happen."

I am simply uncertain how much divine surprise there really can be in an open universe. In response to criticisms like this, the open theist William Hasker seems to back down from the surprise claim. Hasker says that God cannot really be spontaneously reacting to creatures, so even the open theist must take biblical passages about divine surprise to be hyperbolic.[15] The open theist Dean Zimmerman says that "this picture of the workings of divine providence does not require that God ever be *surprised* by the outcomes of the decisions he leaves up to us (though, on their face, some Biblical texts suggest that he has been surprised)."[16] In light of this, it should be unsurprising that I find the *divine surprise* argument unpersuasive.

A Greater Expression of Divine Power. Calvinists and Molinists have long complained that open theism involves a diminishment of divine power and knowledge. I have explained earlier that open theism does not actually diminish God's knowledge. What about divine power? Richard Rice and William Hasker develop some clever responses to this complaint. As Hasker says, the God of open theism "is not less but more than the God of Calvinism."[17] The idea is that there is something more powerful about the God of open theism. To see this, they ask us to consider that God's options are Calvinist universes and open universes.[18] God has it within his power to create either. The overall strategy seems to be this:

1) God can create a Calvinist universe to secure the MCP.

2) God can create an open universe to secure the MCP.

3) God has better reasons to create an open universe than a Calvinist universe.

When it comes to defending (3), Rice and Hasker say that one of God's reasons is a greater expression of divine power. It is common to hear Calvinists say that God can only secure certain goods like the MCP if God fully determines exactly how history will unfold. In which case, the Calvinist is denying (2). The strategy for Rice and Hasker is to say that this is not

---

15. Hasker, "Reply to My Friendly Critics," 214.
16. Zimmerman, "The A-Theory of Time," 792.
17. Hasker, *Providence, Evil, and the Openness of God*, 121.
18. Hasker, *Providence, Evil, and the Openness of God*, 127.

actually God's only option. God can also bring about (2). If that is right, then the modal scope of divine power is actually greater than what the Calvinist says. At this point, the open theist can already say that God has more power than a Calvinist God. From there, Rice and Hasker say that creating an open universe is a greater expression of divine power than creating a Calvinist universe. This way of setting up the debate is clever. It is a good way of fighting back against the standard Calvinist complaints that the God of open theism is limited in power. It makes clear that the God of open theism is greater in power. That is assuming that this argument is successful. I'm not sure about the success of this argument. Here is why.

I will start with the open theist defense of (3). Rice thinks that God has good reasons to prefer an open universe. He gives several reasons. To start, Rice thinks that an open universe gives God a better opportunity to more fully display his power than God would in a Calvinist universe. In a Calvinist universe, God fully controls everything. On the surface, that sounds like an impressive display of divine power, but Rice disagrees. If God allows creatures to have a genuine input into how history unfolds, then God will need to exercise a kind of responsive power that he would not exercise in a Calvinist universe. Also, it seems like God is exercising a particular kind of action when he endows creatures with genuine freedom and the ability to do otherwise. God would not be performing this kind of action in a Calvinist universe.[19] Hence, God displays a greater expression of divine power in creating an open universe.

Calvinists will disagree with Rice. To see the disagreement, let's focus on God's responsive power for a bit. Calvinists might try to maintain that God is responsive to creatures, but open theists will call this into question. God does not actually exercise responsive power on Calvinism since God causally predetermines everything prior to the existence of any creature. I find the open theist position on this point more compelling than the Calvinist. Yet it is worth noting different Calvinist opinions on the matter.

The Calvinist Paul Helm makes some telling remarks in this regard. In some writings, he says that God presents himself as a being who is capable of responding to creatures, though God is not actually responding. Helm says it "is because God wishes people to respond to him that he *must* represent himself to them as one to whom response is possible, as one who acts in time."[20] What is going on here is something called the doctrine of accommodative language. The idea is this: Humans lack the ability to understand God as he really is. So God must condescend when he reveals himself to us.

---

19. Rice, *Future of Open Theism*, 132.
20. Helm, "Impossibility of Divine Passibility," 133–34.

God must reveal himself as the opposite of what he is really like in order to draw us closer to himself. According to John Calvin, "Now the mode of accommodation is for him to represent himself to us not as he is in himself, but as he seems to us."[21] As Helm explains, God wants humans to respond to him, so God must represent himself as a being who is responsive and who reacts to human actions.[22]

Personally, I find this a very bizarre situation. On Helm's view, God is impassible, so it is impossible for God to be moved, caused, or influenced by anything external for his beliefs, emotions, and actions. Though it is metaphysically impossible for God to be responsive and reactive to humans, God intentionally reveals himself as a being who is responsive and reactive. That is a remarkable position to maintain. If that is not divine deception, then I don't know what is. As I have argued elsewhere, this involves ascribing to God the psychological and behavioral profile of a psychopath.[23] Surely that is a clear strike against this view.

But not all Calvinists affirm impassibility. Some affirm that God is passible, and hold a model of God much closer to the one that I have articulated in this book. Rice and Hasker both argue that it is incoherent to affirm divine foreknowledge and passibility. I will be taking up this problem in the next chapter. For now, I will point out a different problem. If God predestines everything in the way that Calvinism says, it still seems like God is not really responsive. The open theist can complain that the Calvinist God is not actually responding to anyone. At best, God is preprogramming his "response" to human actions before the foundations of the world.

As I see it, the open theist needs to be careful with how she pushes this objection. This is because open theists often say that God comes up with an exhaustive contingency plan prior to creation. Before God creates the universe, he develops an exhaustive plan for how he will respond to each possible situation in order to guarantee the success of the MCP. In light of this, a Calvinist could turn around and say, "Ah, I see that you agree with us. God has preprogrammed his response to human actions before the foundation of the world." To be sure, the open theist will argue that God still must wait and see what humans will in fact do before he decides to respond. I think that the open theist can get a lot of traction out of this to argue that God is genuinely responding, whereas God is not genuinely responding on Calvinism. Of course, there are Calvinists who affirm that God is temporal. They will also say that God must wait for humans to actually perform an

---

21. Calvin, *Institutes of the Christian Religion*, I.17.13.
22. Helm, *Providence of God*, 53.
23. Mullins, "Closeness with God."

action before he can respond. Again, I think the open theist can nuance her argument to claim a genuine divine response on open theism and not on Calvinism, but I will not belabor the point. My point is that this is not an easy win on behalf of the open theist.

What about Rice's point concerning creaturely power? As I said before, Rice thinks that in creating an open universe, God is able to give creatures a unique kind of causal power that he could not in a Calvinist universe. Thus, God is able to exercise certain kinds of divine actions that he could not in a Calvinist universe—i.e., the act of giving humans genuine causal power. This is a point that is common among open theists.[24] It is a standard open theist claim that God cannot create a universe with free creatures and causally determine how those creatures will act. In the context of this book, the point looks a little bit different, though it still falls in line with what most open theists claim. If God's goal is to create a universe in which he can offer genuine friendship with creatures, the open theist says that God's only options are open universes.

Again, Calvinists will disagree with this point. Helm says that God gives creatures the power to perform their own actions.[25] So long as the human action is spontaneous (i.e., free to do what she wants) and free from external coercion, then the human agent performs a free action.[26] Helm says that this is brought about through primary and secondary causation.[27] I have my doubts about the coherence of primary and secondary causation. I can't believe it is not occasionalism.

As the history of Christian doctrine develops, theologians distinguished between occasionalism, concurrence, and mere conservation or divine sustaining. What Helm and other Calvinists are wishing to affirm is concurrence. To understand what Helm and others are up to, and why I have my doubts, it will be good to give some quick definitions.

I start with mere conservation or divine sustaining. Julia Jorati says, "Mere conservationists hold that creatures can cause their own actions all by themselves, as long as God conserves them and their causal powers."[28]

---

24. Hasker, *Providence, Evil, and the Openness of God*, 121.

25. Helm, "'Openness' in Compatibilism," 88.

26. Helm, "'Openness' in Compatibilism," 85.

27. I must note a confusion on my part in understanding what Helm actually thinks about this issue. In "'Openness' in Compatibilism," Helm seems quite favorable toward primary and secondary causation. Yet in Helm, *Providence of God*, 181–82, he argues that primary and secondary causation does not actually solve anything. I am uncertain what to make of this. It could very well be the case that Helm has changed his mind over the years.

28. Jorati, "Leibniz on Divine Causation," 123.

On this view, God gives creatures genuine causal power to perform actions. They can do whatever action they wish to perform so long as God continues to sustain them in existence. Typically conservationists will say a bit more, but this is the underlying claim. Most conservationists will also say that creatures can exercise their own causal powers so long as God and no other creature intervene. After all, if I go to steal your wallet, the exercise of my power is thwarted if God or neighbor prevent me from performing that action.

Mere conservation seems pretty straightforward. God gives creatures powers that they can exercise in various ways, end of story. Things become much more complicated when it comes to concurrence and occasionalism. This is because both occasionalists and concurrentists affirm something called Divine Universal Causality (DUC). According to DUC, God not only causes creatures to exist, he also directly and immediately causes their mental states, decisions, and actions to exist.[29] God is even said to cause creaturely actions to be actions! This is often described in terms of instrumental causation. An instrument has no power unless an agent directly and immediately moves it. On this view, we are nothing more than instruments of divine action.[30] This is the classical doctrine of divine universal causality.[31] With that in mind, consider occasionalism.

Jorati says, "Occasionalists hold that God is the sole active or efficient cause of creaturely actions."[32] According to Hugh J. McCann and Jonathan L. Kvanvig, occasionalism is the thesis that God is directly responsible for the existence of things, the characteristics they have, and the changes they undergo.[33] This is because God's perfectly rational actions are always specific, so God must cause all of the specific details of everything to be exactly as they are.[34] Occasionalism is typically taken to be incompatible with human freedom because on occasionalism God is the only genuine agent. If humans are not genuine agents because they don't have any causal power, then there is no sense it talking about them having freedom.

Concurrentism is supposed to be a halfway home between occasionalism and mere conservation. Like occasionalism, concurrentists affirm DUC. Like mere conservation, concurrentists affirm that God gives creatures

---

29. McCann, "Free Will and the Mythology of Causation," 251. Rogers, "Foreknowledge, Freedom, and Vicious Circles," 94–97. Frost, "Three Competing Views," 66.

30. Frost, "Three Competing Views," 69–70.

31. Grant, *Free Will and God's Universal Causality*, 4.

32. Jorati, "Leibniz on Divine Causation," 122.

33. McCann and Kvanvig, "Occasionalist Proselytizer," 588.

34. Jorati, "Leibniz on Divine Causation," 125.

genuine causal power. Yet concurrentism also says that God needs to directly causally contribute to each creaturely action.[35] God has to cause your action to be causally efficacious.[36] Otherwise, your action will not produce any effect at all. The claim is that all creaturely power is insufficient to produce any effect on its own.[37] Hence, why God needs to directly cause each and every creaturely action to be efficacious. To be sure, a conservationist will complain at this point. Medieval theologians like Durand of Saint-Pourcain and Peter John Olivi will say that God did not do a very good job at giving you causal power if God has to cause all of your actions to exist, and cause all of your actions to be causally efficacious.[38] I am deeply sympathetic to this complaint. To tease out this complaint further, consider the following.

DUC is affirmed by both occasionalists and concurrentists. Occasionalism says that God is the only genuine causal agent in existence. Concurrentists say that God gives human persons genuine causal power. Concurrence says that God is the primary cause of everything, and that creatures are secondary causes of some things. However, the affirmation of DUC prevents me from seeing any significant difference between the two views. Here is why. DUC says that God causes everything, including my thoughts, desires, and actions. Why do I exist? God directly causes me to exist. Why do I have the thoughts that I do? God directly causes me to have those thoughts. Why do I have the desires that I do? God directly causes me to have those desires. Why do I perform the actions that I perform? God directly causes me to perform those actions. Could I have performed a different action? Yes, but only if God had directly caused me to perform a different action. Would my actions have any causal efficacy without God directly causing them to be efficacious? No, my actions have no causal efficacy without God directly making it so. This is what DUC says. Notice that this is also precisely what the occasionalist says. So I am left asking, what is the difference between occasionalism and concurrentism? It looks to me like DUC just entails occasionalism. In which case, there is no such thing as human freedom. It will do no good for the concurrentist to say, "God gives creatures genuine causal power," nor will it do any good to invoke secondary causation. On DUC, God directly causes me to have causal power, and God directly causes me to exercise my power in a particular way. Nothing here has changed the analysis of the situation. It is still the case that I only

35. Jorati, "Leibniz on Divine Causation," 123.

36. Webster, "On the Theology of Providence," 164 and 167. Helseth, "God Causes All Things," 31.

37. Tuttle, "Durand and Suarez on Divine Causation," 98.

38. Tuttle, "Durand and Suarez on Divine Causation," 89. Frost, "Three Competing Views," 67.

perform an action because God directly causes me to perform that action. Which is precisely what the occasionalist says. So how is the view not occasionalism? I can't believe it's not occasionalism.

Personally, I do think that the distinction between primary and secondary causation, as it is typically stated, is incoherent. I think it looks exactly like occasionalism. Yet there is another serious concern that I have. James 1:13 says that God does not tempt anyone.[39] It is difficult to understand how God is not tempting me to sin when God is directly causing my thoughts and actions as well as the thoughts and actions of those around me. This raises the common objection that God is the author of sin. Many theologians will reply that God does not directly cause your sinful thoughts and actions, but instead merely permits your sinful thoughts and actions. That is a perfectly fine reply as far as it goes, but it does not work on DUC. Again, DUC says that God is the immediate and direct cause of all creaturely thoughts and actions. If God is merely permitting you to sin, the suggestion is that God is not causing you to sin. In which case, DUC has been abandoned.

For these reasons and others, I agree with Hasker in affirming that mere conservation is all we need.[40] Be that as it may, I find myself less certain that this counts as a point in favor of open theism. Within the context of the present discussion, the open theist is making a very particular point. On her view, the God of open theism can do everything that Calvinism says and more. As Hasker says, the God of open theism "is not less but more than the God of Calvinism."[41] The "more" is create creatures with genuine causal power and freedom. I don't think that is quite right.

The Calvinist says that God gave creatures genuine power and freedom, and that this freedom is compatible with divine determinism. The open theist says that God gave creatures genuine power and freedom, and that this freedom is not compatible with divine determinism. That is not a debate about which God can do more. That is a debate about what is metaphysically possible. If it is metaphysically impossible for freedom and determinism to be compatible, then it is not possible for God to create a Calvinist universe. So the open theist should not be saying, "My God can do everything your God can do, but more." Instead, the open theist should be saying that Calvinist universes are not really an option for God. It is not the case that the open theist God can do everything that a Calvinist God can do

---

39. Thanks to my 2023 students at Palm Beach Atlantic University for pointing out this argument to me.

40. Hasker, "Reply to My Friendly Critics," 215–16.

41. Hasker, *Providence, Evil, and the Openness of God*, 121.

since the claim is that creating a Calvinist universe is not possible. Perhaps it will be helpful to restate the argument.

It looks like Rice and Hasker are saying this:

1) God can create a Calvinist universe to secure the MCP.

2) God can create an open universe to secure the MCP.

3) God has better reasons to create an open universe than a Calvinist universe.

Again, this way of setting up the debate is clever. It is a good way of fighting back against the standard Calvinist complaints that the God of open theism is limited in power. The Calvinist says that (2) is not really an option for God. When Rice and Hasker say that (1) and (2) are options for God, they can maintain that God has more power. After all, more options, more power. However, as the discussion in Rice and Hasker unfolds, it seems like they are really making a very different conclusion. It seems like they are saying something like,

4) A Calvinist universe is impossible because human freedom is not compatible with theological determinism.

That entails,

5) God cannot create a Calvinist universe to secure the MCP.

Which gives us a contradiction when we remember (1).

6) God can create a Calvinist universe to secure the MCP and God cannot create a Calvinist universe to secure the MCP.

The open theist has a contradiction here in her standard argumentative strategy. That is not good. Yet there is an easy fix. The open theist can change her argumentative strategy by rejecting (1). Granted, it does not have the same rhetorical force as, "My God can do everything your God can, but more." This is because the open theist is basically saying the same thing as the Calvinist—there really is only one set of universes for God to consider. However, this argumentative strategy is a more cogent argument because it does not land us in a contradiction.

The Problem of Evil. It is conventional wisdom in contemporary thought that open theists claim an advantage with regards to the problem of evil. Yet this advantage is sometimes misstated or overstated.[42] Sometimes

---

42. For more on this point, see Judisch, "Meticulous Providence and Gratuitous Evil," 65.

people will say that God gets off the hook because God does not know the future. I often find it difficult to discern exactly what is being claimed here. I think it is something like this. On Calvinism, it is difficult to see how God is not the author of evil. Since God is causally responsible for everything that takes place, it really seems like God is the author of evil.[43] God intentionally selected a universe and timeline with the specific evils that we see in the world today. It seems like there must be some very real sense in which God desires the occurrence of those evils! In popular discourse, it sometimes seems like the open theist can avoid saying this since God does not know the future. Since God does not know exactly what will happen when he creates an open universe, God does not intend for those evils to occur. At least that is how the discussion goes in popular discourse.

The reality of the situation is quite different. Open theism cannot so easily get God off the hook like that. To see this, recall the discussion about the general features of a friendly universe. There I discussed the work of several open theist authors, like John Hick and Richard Swinburne. Both of them maintain that if God wants to create a universe where genuine divine-human friendship is possible, then God must create a universe with the real possibility, and in fact inevitability, of suffering. The open theist Keith Ward makes similar remarks. Ward says that when God selects a particular kind of universe, God is desiring to bring about the good things of that universe. God does not desire that suffering take place. So far so good, but notice what else Ward says. Ward admits that the existence of suffering is inevitable given the kind of universe that God wants to create. However, Ward thinks that this is still somewhat better than what the Calvinist can claim. Ward writes,

> God is the source of that suffering, and bears responsibility for it. But it makes a profound difference to the situation if God does not desire it for its own sake, but rather intends that it should be diminished and abolished wherever that is possible, whether by divine or by creaturely action.[44]

For Ward, God does bear some responsibility for bringing about a universe in which suffering is inevitable. Open theists are divided among themselves about how exactly to understand that responsibility. Swinburne maintains that God is within his rights to create such a world, and that God is being generous in giving creatures the opportunity to exist, freely develop a moral character, and enter into friendship with God. Swinburne says that

---

43. Hasker, *Providence, Evil, and the Openness of God*, 130–33.
44. Ward, *Religion and Creation*, 221.

God does take on the responsibility of ensuring that humans have a life that is over all a good one.[45] Hick takes this to imply universalism where every human person eventually agrees to enter into friendship with God.[46] Open theists seem to be divided on this issue. One thing is for sure. Open theists regularly talk about God allowing or permitting particular evils to occur. This is also exactly what Calvinists say when trying to explain how God is not the author of evil. In fact, there are some very sophisticated accounts of divine permission from contemporary Calvinists that I am not entirely sure how to respond to at this point in my life.[47] I will leave it up to you to figure out what to make of all of this. I discuss all of this to make a very minimal point—the open theist does not have an automatic, obvious advantage when it comes to the problem of evil. Open theists must say a great deal more about the problem of evil, just like everyone else.

Pereboom offers an objection related to the problem of evil. Open theists often appeal to the value of human freedom when developing a theodicy. For example, Swinburne says that the efficacy of human freedom is a high intrinsic value that sometimes justifies God in permitting the bad consequences of immoral acts. Following the lead of David Lewis, Pereboom does not think that this is a satisfying explanation for why God permits certain evils. The objection goes like this. When we contemplate preventing someone's evil actions, we do not take into consideration the wrongdoer's freedom. The wrongdoer's freedom is a weightless consideration. If God's reasons for permitting some evils is based on the value of the wrongdoer's freedom, then this undermines our trust in God.[48]

I find myself unpersuaded by objections like this. To start, we often do consider the value of the wrongdoer's freedom in permitting some evils. Parents will often permit their teenagers to do wrong things because they want to allow their child to make her own morally significant decisions. We often have friends who are about to do something morally objectionable. We might advise our friend not to do such things, but we don't go beyond that because we respect our friend's autonomy. Governments are constantly making decisions about which kinds of moral actions they will permit and which they will try to stop. One reason that factors into these decisions is the individual liberty of the citizens. So I think it is simply false that the value of a wrongdoer's freedom is a weightless consideration.

---

45. Swinburne, *Existence of God*, 262. Cf. Swinburne, *Providence and the Problem of Evil*, 224.

46. For the full development of this view, see Hick, *Evil and the Love of God*.

47. Bignon, "Lord Willing and God Forbid."

48. Pereboom, "Theological Determinism and the Relationship with God," 212–13.

Of course, there are certainly cases where the morally objectionable action is so severe that we think an intervention does override any consideration of the wrongdoer's freedom. But consider three things. First, Swinburne's theodicy only says that the intrinsic value of human freedom *sometimes* justifies God in permitting *certain* evils. That is consistent with everything I have said thus far. Second, it is not like Swinburne's entire theodicy is just about humans merely having freedom. Swinburne is clear that God allows for the possibility of certain evils in order to allow for the possibility of greater goods, like friendship with God.[49] For theodicies like Swinburne and Hick, one should expect there to be cases of unnecessary evil, or instances of evil that do not directly serve some greater purpose. This is because a world where creatures can perform significant actions is a world where there are real consequences for creaturely actions. The explanation for why some particular instance of evil occurred is often, "Because some agent chose to do a bad thing," and nothing more. Third, and more importantly, there is a difference between God's obligations and human obligations. The average human has a very limited network of obligations compared to God's. Humans are responsible for those around them, which is always a limited number of people. God, however, is responsible for maintaining an entire universe. This requires a bit more to be teased out.

Standard objections to free will and soul-building theodicies question why God does not intervene more. The idea is that God should be obligated to intervene to prevent all cases of unnecessary suffering.[50] After all, there are some instances of evils that are so terrible that we are obligated to intervene to stop them. Shouldn't the same thing apply to God? I am not entirely certain. I think that if God decides to create humans, then God is obligated to ensure that humans have the ample opportunity to have a life that is, on the whole, one worth living. I think that this involves certain duties on God's part such as providing humans with grace, and opportunities for salvation even after death. I also think that it requires that God create and sustain a universe in which humans can perform morally significant actions. These are actions that could potentially benefit or harm other fellow humans. If God does not sustain an environment in which creatures can perform morally significant actions, then the potential for humans to develop virtuous characters becomes impossible.

There are lots of ways to frustrate the possibility of virtuous character development. Constant divine intervention is one of them. To see this, start with a very general claim: God must prevent all unnecessary evil. How far

---

49. Swinburne, *Existence of God*, 268.
50. Oord, *Pluriform Love*, 160.

should we go with this claim? Should we say that God should prevent every sinful thought? After all, is it really necessary to have a bunch of humans run around with sinful thoughts? Say that God does immediately put a stop to every sinful thought. Every single time someone contemplates doing something sinful, God immediately creates a kind of cognitive dissonance in that person's head. This would surely undermine the entire project of soul-making. This kind of divine intervention would be so pervasive as to become a law of nature. Humans would quickly learn that they cannot think about certain things for even a few seconds. This kind of divine thought policing would not produce any morally virtuous people. No one would think good thoughts for the sake of the good. Instead, they would only be thinking what the nanny state allows. Given this, it would seem that God would need to be a bit more hands off. He cannot be the thought police because that would undermine the very idea of soul-making.

What about some other everyday case of moral wrongdoing? Imagine that you are walking down the street and you see a thief trying to steal an elderly woman's purse. The thief in question is an adolescent who is fairly small, and has no weapons on him. You could easily win a fight with this kid. In this case, it might seem obvious to some that you should try to intervene. You should try to grab the kid to stop him from getting away with the purse. What should God do in this case? Someone like Swinburne might say that God should do nothing in this case because God has given everyone the opportunity to freely develop their moral characters, and God has provided moral instruction through conscience, reason, and special revelation. Any further intervention on God's part would undermine the possibility for human moral character development.

Think about it this way. Imagine that every time someone is about to commit a morally objectionable act, God immediately presses pause. God just calls some sort of cosmic timeout where the person is frozen in place, unable to move for about ten minutes. This is a rather odd world to be sure, but notice the implications of this. The cosmic timeout is so generalized that it is basically a law of nature. Humans will naturally learn that any attempt to do something wrong will lead to a temporary timeout. Their choices will be coerced in the direction of only performing good actions. Given the coercion, they will not develop genuinely virtuous characters.

In response to this, one might complain that this is a bit much. Sure, if God intervened to stop all instances of evil, humans would find themselves with no genuine freedom. But surely there are some cases where God is obliged to intervene. I reply that there might be. I just have no idea what those cases are. Say that God does not have an obligation to stop all instances of evil because that would undermine the possibility of humans developing their own moral character. Perhaps God has an obligation to prevent all cases of really serious evils, like murder. Would that get us anywhere? I say no. If God prevents all cases of murder, then this is a kind of law-like regularity that humans will quickly observe. God's hand will be so clearly seen in ordinary life that humans will be coerced into performing certain kinds of actions.[51] And on we can go if we keep saying, "God is obligated to intervene in all cases of serious evils E."

It would seem that such generalized statements would involve divine actions that undermine the entire possibility of human freedom and character development. I find it plausible that God's network of obligations includes maintaining the possibility of human freedom and character development. This is an obligation that God acquired when he freely decided to create a universe where humans can grow into the kind of beings that can befriend God. If God decides to create a universe like that, he acquires a duty of care to ensure that humans have ample opportunity to build their souls and enter into friendship with God. This moral obligation limits the range of subsequent divine actions that God can perform.

As I see it, God's network of obligations is different from the network of obligations that the average human has. Think of it like this. Say that everyone is obligated to stop all cases of murder in so far as it is possible for them to do so. The average human does not regularly find herself in situations where (i) a murder is happening, and (ii) it is possible for her to do something about it.[52] If the occasion should arise, and she does successfully intervene to stop the murder, she has only undermined a relatively small number of the murderer's free actions, and it does seem that she is justified in doing that. The situation is different with God. God is aware of all the murders taking place in the world. If God always intervenes, then God is regularly undermining the freedom of a significantly large number of humans. This is because God is not simply stopping the individual murderer, but also instructing the rest of humanity that such actions are impossible to perform. The knock-on effects of regular divine intervention are significantly greater in scope than anything that you or I are capable of. That would seem to factor into the network of obligations that God has compared to ours.

To be clear, I am not saying that God never intervenes. For all I know, God could be intervening more often than any of us are aware. My claim is that one of God's obligations is to maintain a universe where significant

---

51. Swinburne, *Existence of God*, 268.

52. I write this sentence in Philadelphia, where I do regularly find myself surrounded by murder, but there is very little that I can do about it.

human freedom is possible. Suggestions that God should regularly intervene often assume that this would be easy for God to pull off. I think that such suggestions are not thinking through the scope of considerations that God has in maintaining a universe, nor the implications of regular divine intervention.

WHY CREATE A MOLINIST UNIVERSE?

As I have discussed above, the Molinist can claim many of the same values as the Calvinist and the open theist. Given Molinism, God doesn't get the surprise of an open universe, but who cares. Given what open theism says about God's amazing predictive power, and the fact that humans tend to be pretty predictable, there really isn't that much divine surprise anyway in an open universe. The Molinist says that God can get the risk-free sovereignty of a Calvinist universe, but with the genuine freedom of an open universe.[53] God can get all the advantages of soul-building and free will theodicies, without having to say that God is taking risks when he creates a universe.[54] Also, Molinism has a straightforward way of explaining God's unfulfilled desires by appealing to things like transworld depravity.[55] This all seems pretty great, and I think one can easily see why Molinism has been so initially attractive to so many people. It seems to get the best of both worlds. Of course, the critics disagree. The critics think that Molinism gets the worst of each view, and some additional problems.

General or Meticulous Providence. Hasker claims that Molinism must adopt a meticulous account of providence. On meticulous providence, God has an exhaustive control over each specific situation. Whatever God intends to bring about for each specific situation will certainly be achieved. God adopts specific-benefit policies for governing the world which would state that every divine act at each moment should achieve a very particular benefit. For example, every instance of evil should be for the purpose of building souls.[56]

Things are allegedly different on a general providence where God sets up the general structures of the universe in order to allow free creatures to have meaningful input in how history unfolds. On general providence,

---

53. For a full defense, see Flint, *Divine Providence.*

54. For a classic account of the free will defense that revived interest in Molinism, see Plantinga, *God, Freedom, and Evil.*

55. Craig, "No Other Name."

56. Hasker, "Open Theist View," 61.

God adopts general-policies for governing the world. God does not have a specific intention for each and every event that takes place in the universe.[57]

When it comes to developing a theodicy, Hasker says that a meticulous account of providence must say that each instance of suffering is permitted by God to bring about some specific benefit. That would seem to make the task of theodicy significantly more difficult in the face of soul-crushing evils.[58] Some instances of evil really do seem pointless, and really do seem to bring about no obvious benefit. Seemingly pointless evils can play a significant role in providing evidence for thinking that God has no such purpose for permitting them, or perhaps even provide evidence that God does not exist.[59] This is what one sees in standard versions of the evidential problem of evil against the existence of God.

This is not an obvious strike against Molinism since there are many responses to the evidential problem of evil from Calvinists, Molinists, and open theists. The point is merely that the Molinist must provide an answer to the evidential problem of evil if she is committed to a meticulous account of divine providence. Someone like Hasker could argue that a general account of providence can accommodate, and in fact expect there to be, pointless instances of evil. In which case, a general account of providence has a much easier time addressing the evidential problem of evil. Seemingly pointless instances of evil are not in fact evidence against the existence of God.

How should the Molinist respond to these considerations? For some Molinists, they will happily accept the meticulous account of providence. A meticulous account of providence is exactly what they want. Others, however, will demure. They want a more general account of providence. Molinists are in luck here. More recent discussions on Molinism have demonstrated that Molinism is actually consistent with a general account of divine providence.[60] God could survey all of the possible Molinist universes, and use general-policies for selecting which universe to create. Just because a Molinist universe contains a specific timeline does not mean that every event in the timeline has some specific benefit for advancing God's goal of achieving the MCP. Molinism does not say that God completely controls everything that happens in any possible universe that he might create.[61] A

---

57. Sanders, *God Who Risks*, 226.
58. Hasker, "Open Theist Theodicy of Natural Evil," 285.
59. Cf. Rowe, *God and the Problem of Evil*.
60. Judisch, "Meticulous Providence and Gratuitous Evil." Cf. Craig, "Molinist View," 143.
61. Judisch, "Meticulous Providence and Gratuitous Evil," 81.

Molinist universe could contain seemingly random events that do not bring about any specific benefit for anyone.

As I see it, it seems like an advantage to Molinism that it can accommodate both a meticulous and a general account of providence. This certainly helps bolster the Molinst claim that she can enjoy the best of both Calvinist and open universes.

Occasionalism. Luis de Molina affirmed the distinction between primary and secondary causation that I discussed above with Calvinism. Molina also affirms the doctrine of concurrence. At least he claims to affirm concurrence. He actually makes some modifications to the doctrine. With the previous account, God has to directly act on a human agent to cause the agent to perform her own action. God has to cause you to cause things. That looks like occasionalism. Molina takes a different route, and denies that God has to cause you to cause things.[62] At first glance, it seems like God is simply causally sustaining you in existence. Molina will deny that this is merely divine conservation. Molina says that God's concurrence is neutral in that it does not cause creatures to do any particular action. Yet there is supposed to be some sense in which God acts directly on the effect of the agent instead of on the agent herself.[63]

Personally, I find this very bizarre. Sure, it is not exactly the occasionalism that I discussed above, but it still seems to be in the neighborhood. God is not causing you to cause things, but God is causally bringing about the effects of your action. That seems like your action is not really all that efficacious. In which case the specter of occasionalism comes back. You are not really a causal agent if you cannot causally bring about effects. If God has to bring about the effects of your action, then it seems like you don't have an efficacious will.

Perhaps Molinism doesn't really need this doctrine of concurrence. As far as I can tell, Molinism just needs divine sustaining. Any doctrine of concurrence seems like too much. It is one thing to speak of God allowing or permitting a creature's actions, and another to speak of God causing the actions of a creature or causing the effects of a creature. I think that the doctrine of concurrence is not what most theologians really want, but I am basing my opinion on the never-ending vague statements that I encounter in the average theology textbook.

Some will complain that mere divine sustaining is deism. Without concurrence, we would be living in a deistic world. I don't find this complaint persuasive in the slightest. Say that God is merely sustaining us in

---

62. Molina, *On Divine Foreknowledge*, 18.
63. Molina, *On Divine Foreknowledge*, 18.

existence. Also say that God sometimes answers prayers, gives people grace, intervenes to perform a miracle here and there, becomes incarnate in Jesus Christ, and indwells in believers. Is that deism? If it is deism, it is a very funny sort of deism that looks just like biblical Christianity.

As I see it, there is no need to say that God must cause your causings, nor that God must cause your effects. God just needs to keep us in existence in order for us to perform free actions. That is an advantage over Calvinism. It seems difficult for the open theist to complain about this rewrite too since they are clearly not interested in affirming universal divine causality or concurrence. So once again, it seems like Molinism gets the best of Calvinism and open theism, without the disadvantage of occasionalism, and without the disadvantage of risky business.

Grounding Objection. Is middle knowledge possible? I don't know. I hope so, but there is something called the grounding objection to Molinism.[64] It can go a little something like this. Propositions are the ultimate bearers of truth. A proposition is true when it accurately describes the world as being a certain way. A proposition is false when it fails to accurately describe the way the world is. In stating things in this way, there is some sort of relationship between truth and the world. There are several seemingly plausible principles that philosophers adopt to capture the relationship between truth and the world. In particular, there is a plausible assumption that the truth of a proposition depends for its truth on the world.[65] The intuition here is the notion that truth supervenes on being (TSB). This can be defined as follows:

> TSB: Truth supervenes on things and how things are.[66]

The idea of (TSB) is supposed to be that whatever is true cannot float free from the way that the world is. This is said to undergird the truthmaker principle. This can be defined as follows:

> Truthmaking (TM): A proposition is true because there exists something that makes it true.

In light of (TM), many philosophers have engaged in something called the *truthmaking project* which is the task of finding those things in the world that make various propositions true.[67]

---

64. Hasker, "(Non-) Existence of Molinist Counterfactuals."
65. For an extended discussion see Armstrong, *Truth and Truthmakers*.
66. Kierland and Monton, "Presentism and the Objection from Being-Supervenience," 487.
67. Cameron, *Moving Spotlight*, 103.

Critics of Molinism say that there are no truthmakers for the counterfactuals of creaturely freedom prior to God's decision to create. Prior to creation, when God existed all alone, there are no creatures to ground the truths about what these creatures would or would not do. What could possibly ground the truths about what creatures would do in any possible circumstance?

Molinists have various replies. Some might say that the essences of creatures ground these truths.[68] I think that is a line of reasoning worth pursuing, but I am unpersuaded that this strategy can avoid some sort of necessitarianism or determinism. My preferred strategy is different. I think that these objections to Molinism rely on some controversial philosophical assumptions about truth supervening on being and truthmaker theory. Without going into too much detail, I think that there is good reason to reject these claims.[69] I do not think that truth supervenes on being, nor do I think that there need to be presently existing entities to ground the truths of the world. As John Leslie explains,

> Truths *do not* always need "truthmakers" among actually existing things. If you and I exist as parts of a four-dimensional block, and if the entire block suddenly vanished, and if any other existing things all vanished as well, then it would of course still be true that you and I had once existed. Nothing whatever could suddenly make it true that you and I had never existed. The sole truthmaker needed for a thing's once having existed is *that thing's once having existed*, period.[70]

I reject truthmaker theory, and that seems to help the Molinist out quite a bit. At least that is how Trenton Merricks understands the situation. According to Merricks there just are certain counterfactuals of creaturely freedom that are true.[71] There is nothing more to say. As one might expect, critics of Molinism do not like Merricks's position because they think that truthmaker theory is more plausible. Hasker refers to Merricks's rejection of truthmaker as a "radical" solution to the grounding objection against Molinism.[72] As I see it, this is not actually a radical solution. The rejection of truthmaker theory has strong support from philosophers quite independent of any theological considerations. Jonathan Tallant argues that truthmaker theory is incoherent and implausible because it cannot adequately account

---

68. MacGregor, *Molinist Philosophical and Theological Ventures*, ch. 3.
69. Merricks, *Truth and Ontology*.
70. Leslie, "Way of Picturing God," 52.
71. Merricks, "Truth and Molinism."
72. Hasker, "(Non-) Existence of Molinist Counterfactuals," 29.

WHY CREATE ANY PARTICULAR UNIVERSE? 123

for obvious truths like negative existentials, truths about the past and future, and so on.[73] Even open theists like Patrick Todd reject truthmaker theory for reasons similar to that as Leslie noted above.[74]

A growing number of philosophers are pointing out that principles like (TSB) are not actually as intuitive as they initially appear. Fabrice Correia and Sven Rosenkranz point out that the (TSB) has a rather odd consequence. In order for a statement to satisfy the (TSB), the (TSB) requires the existence of all sorts of unexpected things that the statement itself never mentions. Why should the truth of any given statement require grounding by something that the statement itself does not even claim or assert exists?[75]

Correia and Rosenkranz ask us to consider the proposition <Nero was mad>. When one utters this statement, what exactly are they asserting? Are they asserting that the moments of time at which Nero is located exist just as much as the present moment of time exists? That seems doubtful, but truthmaker pushes us to say yes. Moreover, Correia and Rosenkranz point out that the mere existence of past moments is insufficient to ground the truth of <Nero was mad> given the requirements of the (TSB). One will also need to build in some entities like tropes, or events, or temporal counterparts, and so on.[76] For example, the eternalist asks us to build in temporal counterparts. Eternalism is an ontology of time that says past, present, and future moments of time all exist. Temporal counterparts are numerically distinct objects that are located at specific moments. They are said to have interesting causal relations between them that allow one to say that there is some stretched sense in which they are the "same" object. If you are unable to follow all of this, don't worry. That is partly my point; things have already started to go off the rails, and we still have not yet satisfied the seemingly intuitive (TSB). Elsewhere I have explained just how odd these entities are, and how they undermine any notion of Christian salvation and life after death.[77] Here I simply want to note that affirming the existence of such things is rather extravagant and counterintuitive. When one asserts <Nero was mad> is she asserting that past moments are on an ontological par with the moment of this utterance, and at these past moments there exist a series of numerically distinct temporal Nero counterparts that are instantiating properties like *madness*? I suppose that a consistent eternalist will be asserting such things, but I doubt very much that the rest of us are

73. Tallant, *Truth and the World*.
74. Todd, *Open Future*, 15–16.
75. Correia and Rosenkranz, *Nothing to Come*, 107.
76. Correia and Rosenkranz, *Nothing to Come*, 107.
77. Mullins, "Identity through Time and Personal Salvation."

implying anything of the sort when we say <Nero was mad>. Instead, most people would simply be saying that the past was a certain way.

Ulrich Meyer makes a general comment about the entire truthmaking project. He writes that,

> instead of ensuring metaphysical honesty, the truthmaker principle tends to generate more extravagant philosophical views than it eliminates.... The truthmaker principle codifies a preference for a certain type of metaphysical theory rather than providing a neutral court of appeal in which rival philosophical views can be adjudicated.[78]

I think that the case against truthmaker theory is significantly stronger than the critics of Molinism seem to admit. Hence, I am reluctant to feel the force of the grounding objection against Molinism as it is standardly discussed.

Divine and Human Freedom. I wish to raise one more issue that baffles me. As I have mentioned before, Molinism says that there are no truths about what God would do prior to his decision to create in general. It seems odd to me that there are no true counterfactuals of divine freedom prior to God's creative decision, but that there are true counterfactuals of human freedom prior to God's creative decision. Alfred J. Freddoso says that this is "the weakest link in the Molinist chain."[79] If Molinism is willing to allow these for humans, then why not for God? Something seems off here, but I have yet to put my finger on exactly what is off.

Luis de Molina's own explanation is that if God foreknew his own actions before he decided to create or not create, then God would not have free will.[80] This should be worrying for the Molinist. If God would not be free in this case, then how can humans be free with God foreknowing their actions before they have made their choices? In defense of Molina, Kirk R. MacGregor says that if an agent foreknows his own actions before he makes a decision, then he is not free. Yet it is not a problem for freedom if someone else foreknows the agent's action because merely foreknowing does not cause the agent's act.[81] In other words, if you foreknow your own actions, then you don't have free will, but it is no big deal if someone else foreknows your actions. When it comes to the case of God, it would only be a problem for divine freedom if God foreknew his creative action before he had decided to create. Yet, it is no problem for God to foreknow your

---

78. Meyer, *Nature of Time*, 54–55.
79. Molina, *On Divine Foreknowledge*, 53.
80. Molina, *On Divine Foreknowledge*, 171.
81. MacGregor, *Molinist Philosophical and Theological Ventures*, 53–54.

actions because his foreknowledge does not cause you to do whatever it is that you do.

Something does not seem quite right here. On this line of reasoning, one better hope that God never tells you what you are going to do in the future. If God did tell you, then you would foreknow your actions before you have made a decision. In which case, you would not be free! So in order to preserve your freedom, it would seem that God must refrain from informing humans of their future actions.

Yet surely that cannot be right. If there is a problem for freedom, I should think that the problem would be the fact that what you will do in the future is completely settled before you make any decisions. Your knowledge or ignorance of this settled future seems irrelevant to me. Say that it is a completely settled matter that you will finish reading this book tomorrow at 2:03 p.m. Your knowledge or ignorance of this fact does not change this fact's settled status. Why would simply knowing this fact undermine your freedom? If you know it or you don't, either way, it is already settled what you will do.

It seems to me that MacGregor's defense of Molina dances around the underlying problem. Molina is not worried about God merely foreknowing what his own actions will be. No, not at all. Molina says that before God decides to create, there is no fact of the matter about what God will do. There is no settled future for God because if there were, God would not be free. It seems to me that Molina understands that the real problem for divine freedom is not foreknowledge, but rather the settled future.

The problem of freedom and a settled future is a complicated one, and I have nothing more of interest to say about it at this time because others have addressed it better than I can.[82] Again, this book is about exploring where I currently am in my understanding of God. I don't have all the answers. In forcing my theological musings on you, I hope that you may one day help me figure out how to address some of these issues.

WHICH KIND OF UNIVERSE WOULD GOD CREATE? CAN OMNISUBJECTIVITY HELP?

The above considerations might not seem to lead in any particular direction. The case for God to pick any particular kind of universe does not seem to be as decisive as one might hope. In the final section of this chapter, I want to consider one proposal for tilting the scales in the direction of Molinist universes.

82. Byerly, *Mechanics of Divine Foreknowledge and Providence*.

Linda Zagzebski has claimed that omnisubjectivity can help us tackle the general and particular problems of creation. I disagree, but before saying why, I need to explain Zagzebski's view. Zagzebski takes omnisubjectivity to be God's total perfect empathy of all creaturely conscious states. To remind everyone, empathy is gained by having a direct cognitive acquaintance with another person. Thus it seems a bit difficult to figure out how empathy could help God decide which kind of universe to create. When God is deciding, there are no creatures in existence for God to empathize with.

Zagzebski is not deterred by this problem, and suggests that God might have counterfactual or hypothetical omnisubjectivity. Any Molinist might initially find this attractive because it looks like an extension of middle knowledge. This is divine empathy with merely possible conscious states of merely possible conscious creatures. Zagzebski claims that this kind of power better captures God's cognitive perfection.[83] Not only that, she thinks that it would help us make sense of God's creation and providential control. She writes,

> The ability to grasp counterfactual conscious states from a first person perspective seems to be a necessary condition for ideal governance of the world. If God does not know what it would be like for conscious beings to have their experiences, how can God know what to create?[84]

On standard accounts of God's omniscience and decision to create, theologians only speak of God knowing the truthvalues of the propositions about those possible universes. God is said to know all of the descriptive facts about those possible worlds, but there is hardly any mention of God knowing the phenomenal facts about what those worlds are like. Zagzebski takes this to be a cognitive deficiency that is unbefitting of God. She says,

> Lacking a grasp of those experiences as they would be experienced by individual beings in that world is a failure to fully grasp that world, and hence, it is a failure to grasp the ways the actual world could have turned out. That does not seem worthy of a cognitively perfect being.[85]

When it comes to discerning which particular universe God should create, Zagzebski says that God's counterfactual omnisubjectivity must come into play. God's empathetic knowledge will help him compare and contrast the different possible universes that he might create. Without such

---

83. Zagzebski, *Omnisubjectivity*, 36.
84. Zagzebski, *Omnisubjectivity*, 36.
85. Zagzebski, *Omnisubjectivity*, 36.

knowledge, she can't see how God could adequately compare the universes. She asks us to imagine that God lacks counterfactual omnisubjectivity. In that case, God "could not know what it would be like for him to create such a world and to have an empathic awareness of it. This not only puts serious limitations on a creator God, but also limits his knowledge of his own counterfactual self."[86] This, says Zagzebski, is a serious problem.

She doesn't say much about how all of this works, but she does give some suggestions.[87] For example, she asks us to consider the notion that God rewards and punishes free creatures. Zagzebski says that if God does not know in advance what it would be like for a person to have certain subjective experiences, then it is difficult to see how God could adequately have a plan for rewarding and punishing people.[88]

What are we to make of all of this? I have my doubts that this is coherent. Again, omnisubjectivity is total perfect empathy. Empathy is had by way of a direct cognitive acquaintance with another conscious being. In the scenarios that Zagzebski is describing, there are no conscious creatures for God to empathize with. So this entire suggestion seems to be a nonstarter. However, there is something in the neighborhood that might help—simulation. Simulation is one method that we use for trying to empathize with others, but it is not the same thing as empathy. Simulation is when you try to imagine what it might be like for someone to undergo a particular experience in a particular situation. We do this all the time, and it can be quite useful. However, this is not the exact same as actually empathizing with someone because empathy involves an actual, direct, cognitive acquaintance with another person.

Simulation also is not the same as actually undergoing a particular experience. Consider the case of so-called transformative experiences, like having a child. It is one thing to imagine what it might be like to have a child, and quite another to actually have a child. Transformative experiences are said to be cases where it is impossible to really know what it will be like prior to undergoing the experience itself.

I say that the same applies to God. Prior to creation, God may be able to simulate what it would be like to create a universe, but that is not the same as actually experiencing what it is like to create a universe. Prior to creation, God just cannot know what that actual experience is like. The same goes for God contemplating his ideas and simulating all the possible combinations

---

86. Zagzebski, *Omnisubjectivity*, 37–38.

87. As of this writing, I have read some earlier drafts of her forthcoming book on omnisubjectivity. In this new book, Zagzebski promises to develop the details in full.

88. Zagzebski, *Omnisubjectivity*, 38.

of conscious experiences. It is one thing to contemplate the idea of Socrates's emotional life, and quite another to actually empathize with the emotional life of an actually existing Socrates. A cognitively perfect being can tell the difference between a simulation and actuality. As far as I can tell, at best, simulation would only give God phenomenal knowledge of what it might be like for a creature to experience such and such. It would not give God knowledge of what it would actually be like for a creature to experience such and such. So while I think that divine simulation may help some with God's decision about what to create, I think that this suggestion only goes so far.

It is also worth noting that this weaker simulation thesis provides no advantage for Molinism. This is because God could simulate what it would be like to create Calvinist and open universes. So whatever limited benefit simulation might have for the particular problem of creation, it does not obviously point God in any particular direction.

CONCLUDING THOUGHTS

I started this chapter by saying that I am uncertain which kind of universe God has created. After exploring some of the reasons for and against each kind of universe that God might create, I am hoping that you can find my uncertainty understandable, even if not decisive. Perhaps after reading this chapter, you find yourself convinced of a particular view. Maybe you have found ways to deal with the objections I consider, or strengthen the arguments that I offer. If you are uncertain like me, I hope that you will keep pondering the issue in the search for clear answers.

8

The Problem of Foreknowledge and Passibility

IN THIS FINAL CHAPTER, I want to consider one more problem that has bothered me in my own journey to understand God. This is the Problem of Foreknowledge and Passibility.[1] My guess is that many people reading will wonder why I am not discussing the Problem of Foreknowledge and Human Freedom. For many, that seems like a much more difficult problem. If God knows the future, how can humans have free will? To be honest, I don't know how humans can have free will if God knows the future. There are many excellent books written on this topic.[2] After surveying these books and many other sources, I find myself uncertain what to say. There are many answers to the freedom/foreknowledge problem that I find unsatisfying, yet I also don't think that it is obvious that mere foreknowledge undermines human freedom. It depends on other contributing factors. Personally, I am less inclined toward theological determinism because I do not think that determinism is compatible with human freedom. Yet, as I have already admitted, there are some incredibly interesting arguments for the compatibility of theological determinism and human freedom.[3] Basically, I feel that I need to do a great deal more study to make up my mind on this issue.

---

1. I am greatly in debt to Mike DeVitto and Tyler McNabb for pushing me to think through these issues.

2. Byerly, *Mechanics of Divine Foreknowledge and Providence*. Vicens and Kittle, *God and Human Freedom*. Florio and Frigerio, *Divine Omniscience and Human Free Will*.

3. Furlong, *Challenges of Divine Determinism*.

What I want to do in this chapter is explore a different issue that has not received as much attention. This is the Problem of Foreknowledge and Passibility. I am thoroughly convinced that God is passible. God is capable of being moved and influenced by creatures to some extent. God is capable of having a wide range of emotional responses to the world that are consistent with his perfect goodness and rationality. Also, God is capable of having maximal empathy with his creatures. Yet, I am also unwilling to give up God's exhaustive foreknowledge at this point. There are some people who think that I cannot affirm passibility and foreknowledge. I disagree. In this chapter, I will explain why I disagree. Before considering the argument, I need to set the stage by considering some different issues related to omniscience, time, and emotions.

OMNISCIENCE, TIME, AND EMOTION

The objection that I will be considering focuses on an alleged incompatibility between foreknowledge and passibility. I need to set the stage because the different arguments claim that there is something incoherent about the emotional life of a being with infallible knowledge of the future. The arguments have many different unspoken assumptions that need to be brought to the surface. I will start with passibility and then turn to omniscience.

A person is passible if her beliefs, emotions, and actions are moved, caused, or influenced by things external to herself. I say that God is passible because God's beliefs, emotions, and actions are influenced by things external to himself. I take this to be obvious. God's belief that you are sinning is influenced by the fact that you are sinning. God's anger at your sin is also influenced by the fact that you are sinning. God's act to punish you is influenced by the fact that you are sinning. Only someone corrupted by the history of Christian theology could think that it is impossible for God's beliefs, emotions, and actions to be influenced by external things.

In an earlier chapter, I explained that God has maximal cognitive power. This entails the ability to infallibly know all the facts there are, as well as the ability to have perfect rationality, maximal empathy, and so on. My account of God's cognitive perfection is richer than standard accounts of omniscience. On standard accounts of omniscience, God is said to know of the truthvalues of all propositions. For any proposition p, God knows that it has a truthvalue of true or false. Standard accounts of omniscience are purely propositional. They do not typically include the distinct category of experiential or phenomenal knowledge such as knowledge of what it is like to have certain kinds of experiences. As I stated before, experiential knowledge is not reducible to propositional knowledge. This is because you can know that something is the case without knowing what it is like to experience it. For example, I can know that the rain in Spain falls mostly on the plain. This is distinct from knowing what it is like to experience the rain in Spain falling on the plain.

As I see things, omniscience is not the fundamental perfection. Instead, maximal cognitive power is the perfection, and this entails omniscience, but it also entails the ability to have experiential knowledge. This will be important to know as it will come up in the objection to my view.

Say you are like me, and you are strongly inclined to affirm that God has an exhaustive knowledge of the future. Say you are also like me and you are uncertain if you should affirm theological determinism or Molinism. What exactly are you saying about God's foreknowledge?

As I have explained before, foreknowledge depends upon God creating a particular kind of universe with a settled future. The future is settled in the sense that there are propositions that describe what will happen. Foreknowledge concerns a certain set of temporal propositions about the future. Yet there are allegedly two kinds of temporal propositions to consider. These are tensed and tenseless facts.

A tensed fact is a temporal fact that is described using tensed propositions. Tensed propositions describe the world by using statements with *past*, *present*, and *future* tenses. In particular, tensed propositions attempt to describe reality by referring to an objective present moment of time, or the now. For example, consider the tensed propositions <It is now raining>, <It was raining>, and <It will rain>. A tenseless fact describes the world using tenseless propositions. Tenseless propositions describe the world by ordering moments of time in relations of earlier-than, later-than, and simultaneous with. Tenseless propositions do not describe reality by referring to an objective present moment of time. For example, consider the tenseless propositions <It rains at 2 p.m. on July 21, 2020> and <July 21, 2020, is earlier-than July 22, 2020>.

Tensed and tenseless propositions are not reducible to each other because they offer different descriptions of the world. There was a period in the late 1900s where philosophers attempted to reduce tensed propositions to tenseless propositions. This is sometimes known as the detensing project. That is a long and boring story, but most philosophers have concluded that tensed and tenseless propositions cannot be reduced to one another. Today, we are left with a debate over which temporal propositions are needed to give an ideal description of the world.

If you want to give an exhaustive description of temporal reality, which kinds of temporal propositions would you need to use? A tensed theory of time says that an ideal description of the world utilizes both tensed and tenseless propositions, whereas a tenseless theory of time says that an ideal description of the world only utilizes tenseless propositions.[4]

This debate has had an impact on contemporary understandings of divine foreknowledge, though I think it is greatly misguided. Those who affirm that God is timeless regularly rely on the tenseless theory of time in order to avoid having God's knowledge change. One of the features of tensed propositions is that they change their truthvalue depending on what is happening right now. Things are said to be different with tenseless propositions which allegedly do not change their truthvalue. A common claim is that the tenseless theory of time is a theological advantage to any view that affirms divine timelessness. To illustrate this point, consider the following example.

Take the tensed propositions <Ryan is sitting on Arthur's Seat> and <Ryan will sit on Arthur's Seat.> When I wake up in the morning, the proposition <Ryan is sitting on Arthur's Seat> is false. That is not what I am doing at present. At present, I am lying in my bed contemplating the tragedy of having to wake up in the morning. At this point in the day, the proposition <Ryan will sit on Arthur's Seat> is true. Yet, as the day goes on, I walk up to Arthur's Seat, sit down, and take in the marvelous view of Edinburgh. The proposition <Ryan will sit on Arthur's Seat> is no longer true. That proposition is now false. The proposition <Ryan is sitting on Arthur's Seat> becomes true. These temporal propositions change their truthvalues in accordance to the way the world is at present.

Tenseless propositions allegedly do not change their truthvalue. Consider the proposition <Ryan sits on Arthur's Seat at 2 p.m. on May 18, 2021>. Now think about the previous story. When I wake up in my bed on the morning of May 18, 2021, that proposition is true. When I later sit on top of Arthur's Seat, that proposition does not become true because it already is true. As I walk down the mountain back to my home, the proposition remains true. The standard claim is that for all eternity, the proposition <Ryan sits on Arthur's Seat at 2 p.m. on May 18, 2021> is true. The truthvalue of this proposition does not change because it makes no reference to the way the world is at present.

If you affirm the tenseless theory of time, you are saying that the only temporal propositions you need to fully describe the world are tenseless propositions. If you are like me, and you affirm the tensed theory of time, you will be saying that a full description of the temporal world cannot be captured by tenseless propositions alone. A full description of the temporal world must also include tensed propositions as well. There are several

---

4. Pearson, *Rationality, Time, and Self*, 16.

reasons for thinking that the tensed theory is true. I will mention four. The first reason is one that I have never seen discussed before. The other three reasons are commonly discussed, but important for understanding the argument against foreknowledge and passibility.

First, the tenseless theory is inconsistent with Calvinism and Molinism. Recall that the truthvalues of tenseless propositions do not change. That is the standard claim about tenseless propositions within the philosophy of time. This is why many theologians who affirm timelessness and immutability wish to affirm the tenseless theory of time. They think that it will allow them to affirm that God changelessly knows all of the temporal facts about reality. What all contemporary theologians seem to have overlooked is the inconsistency of this with the standard claims from Calvinism and Molinism. Listen to what the Calvinist William Shedd says: "The Divine decree is the necessary condition of the Divine foreknowledge. If God does not first decide what shall come to pass, he cannot know what will come to pass."[5] Recall that on both Calvinism and Molinism, God initially faces an open future. At the so-called moment of natural knowledge, God does not know what will happen in the future because God has not yet decided to create or not create. If the standard description of God's moment of natural knowledge is accurate, then God faces an open future. If God faces an open future, then tenseless propositions like <Ryan sits on Arthur's Seat at 2 p.m. on May 18, 2021> are not true. Those propositions only become true subsequent to God's decision to create in general, and subsequent to God's decision to create a particular universe with a settled future. That is not consistent with the tenseless theory's claim that tenseless propositions do not change their truthvalue.

I anticipate that many Calvinists and Molinists who affirm divine timelessness will not like this. They will say, "Those tenseless propositions are not true, but only from the logical moment of natural knowledge. They are eternally true at the logical moment of free knowledge, so they never switch their truthvalue." I find this to be confused. This is what these people are saying. From all eternity that proposition is both true and false. From God's single timeless moment, it is true that <Ryan sits on Arthur's Seat at 2 p.m. on May 18, 2021>, but somehow it is also false from some logical moment embedded within God's single timeless moment. That is incredibly difficult to make sense of. I strongly suspect that this is nothing but playing with words. In fact, the history of Christian theology is rather interesting on this point. Various theologians have used these logical moments embedded within God's timeless moment in an attempt to solve different theological

---

5. Shedd, *Dogmatic Theology*, 396–97.

puzzles. When they are challenged about these logical moments, it is standard to see these theologians say that this talk of logical moments is nothing more than notions in our heads. It is just a way of talking that helps us make sense of theology, but it does not actually describe anything true about God. For example, when Moses Amyraut was questioned about his particular logical order of God's decrees, he said that the order of decrees is only a distinction within human reason. In God, the decree is one eternal moment without succession of thought, order, priority, or posteriority. In other words, the decree is one eternal act in God without distinction.[6] If that is the case, then all of this talk about logical moments in the life of God is nothing more than a fiction, the use of which is questionable at best. Either way, nothing here helps to show a compatibility between the tenseless theory of time and traditional doctrines of providence.

There is a second reason for thinking that the tenseless theory of time is false. The tenseless theory of time leaves us with an incomplete description of the temporal world. As I mentioned in an earlier chapter, I think that presentism is obviously true. The present moment of time is the only moment that is real. Past moments no longer exist, and future moments do not yet exist. No description of the temporal world can be complete without mentioning what is happening at the present. The tenseless theory of time avoids mentioning the present, thus leaving us with an incomplete description of reality.

Third, the tenseless theory of time makes the practicalities of daily life wildly impractical.[7] This is because practical decision making consistently relies on tensed facts. To see this, consider the following: Imagine I dare you to live like a consistent tenseless theorist for a day. You are only allowed to rely on tenseless propositions to navigate your way throughout your daily business. Can you consistently pull this off without relying on any tensed propositions? If I were a betting man, I would put good money on you failing miserably. To see why, consider a few obstacles that one might face. Imagine that you wake up in the morning knowing that you have a meeting at 10:30 a.m. You also know that you need to leave your house at precisely 9:30 a.m. in order to get to the meeting on time. Here is the first obstacle you will have to face. You will need to know what time it is right now to figure out if you should leave your house sooner than later. The problem is that you are not allowed to rely on tensed facts like what time it is right now. You need to figure out when to leave without relying on tensed facts. That is going to be difficult to say the least. Here is another challenge. Imagine

---

6. Amyraut, *Amyraut on Predestination*, 167.
7. Cf. Pearson, *Rationality, Time, and Self*, 146–47.

THE PROBLEM OF FOREKNOWLEDGE AND PASSIBILITY   135

that your partner says to you, "What are you doing right now?" You are going to have to respond with something like, "Darling, I have explained to you before, there are no tensed facts in the world. Could you rephrase the question without any tenses?" If your partner is inclined to indulge your philosophical proclivities, they might reply, "Sorry. Can you explain to me what you are doing simultaneously with the utterance of this question?" If your partner is not inclined to indulge your philosophical proclivities, I would imagine that the response will be more colorful. The more colorful response accurately tracks the implausibility of the tenseless theory of time.

Fourth, the tenseless theory is inconsistent with the rationality of emotions. This point is going to be important for the argument that I will be considering in later sections, so I will discuss this issue in more detail. As I have said before, emotions can be rational or irrational. It depends on how well an emotion tracks the values in the world in terms of the appropriateness of the emotion type and the fittingness of the intensity of the emotion. For example, if a stranger is not paying attention and bumps into you on the sidewalk, certain emotion types seem fitting. Perhaps annoyance or anger would be appropriate. It depends on how hard they bumped you. Say that the bump is sufficient to justify the emotion of anger, but it is insufficient to justify a fit of rage. The intensity of the anger needs to be appropriate to the offense.

Notice something important about this example. The emotion here is a response to a tensed fact. It is a response to something that is happening right now. The emotion is also justified by a tensed fact. What explains the rationality of the emotion in this case is what is happening right now. The reality is that most of our emotions are about tensed facts. Our emotions concern our present situation, and our present situation is embedded with all sorts of tensed facts about what is happening right now, what has happened, and what will happen. To give some examples, someone might be grieving because of the recent loss of a loved one. Another person will be happy because of their recent acceptance into university. A different person will be anxious about an upcoming exam. These are emotions about tensed facts embedded in our present situation. These emotions are justified by the existence of tensed facts.

This is a serious problem for the tenseless theory of time because the tenseless theory says that there are no tensed facts. Thus, the tenseless theory of time cannot capture the rationality of emotions because most of our emotions are justified by tensed facts. As Olley Pearson points out,

> Many emotions have a temporal orientation. Relief is orientated towards the past. It is appropriate to be relieved that a discomfort

has ended but it is inappropriate to be relieved that a discomfort *will end*. In a connected manner, it is inappropriate to have a tenseless emotion of relief because in such tenseless relief one will not know whether or not the discomfort has ended.[8]

Think of the problem this way. Have you ever had a justified emotion about a tensed fact? Perhaps you have relief that a painful doctor's visit is over. If you have ever had a justified emotion about a tensed fact like that, the tenseless theory of time is false. It is false because the tenseless theory says that there are no tensed facts to justify your emotions. Since I think it is obvious that you have had justified emotions about tensed facts, I think it is obvious that the tenseless theory of time is false.

It would be good to summarize what I have just discussed. There are four takeaways from this discussion that will be helpful to keep in mind as I consider different problems for theological determinism and Molinism. First, God is passible in that God's beliefs, emotions, and actions are influenced by things external to himself. Second, God's omniscience concerns propositions, but that God's cognitive perfection extends beyond that to include experiential knowledge. Third, God's foreknowledge concerns tensed propositions about what will happen in the future. Fourth, emotions are rationally justified by tensed facts.

SOME PROBLEMS FOR THEOLOGICAL DETERMINISM AND MOLINISM

There are two kinds of problems that I want to consider for the theological determinist and Molinist. First, why would God create anything at all? Second, why would God feel anything at all? Both of these problems are often posed by the open theist against anyone who affirms that God has exhaustive foreknowledge of the future.

With regards to the first problem, the Calvinist John Feinberg puts the objection like this:

> A God who has planned everything in advance must be very bored with history. Since he already has planned and knows what will happen, why even bother playing out the script? Only when there is uncertainty because things are not set in advance can our history be of any real interest to God.[9]

Feinberg has a ready reply to this objection. He writes,

---

8. Pearson, *Rationality, Time, and Self*, 28.
9. Feinberg, *No One Like Him*, 801.

Why would God want to go through history with us as it unfolds when he already knows everything he and we will do? For the same reason that the person who meticulously plans every detail of a business meeting or a worship service still wants to attend. For the same reason that someone who knows all the lines of every actor in a play still wants to experience the live performance. Knowing intellectually the blueprint for what will happen cannot take the place of experiencing the actual occurring of everything that is planned. As we saw in nuancing the divine attribute of omniscience, there is a difference between propositional knowledge and experiential knowledge. God's knowing propositionally everything that will occur because he has foreordained it cannot take the place of experiencing history's flow as it passes. Knowing that I will seek his help in time of trial and that he will respond cannot take the place of actually hearing me pray and then responding to my need. No, the "doing" of history is not boring for the king who has planned each moment of it.[10]

This reply seems right to me, and I will elaborate the point further on behalf of determinists like Feinberg. When it comes to God's decree, God's decree seems to be doing several different things. First, it settles truthvalues for tensed propositions about the universe that God is going to create. The decree contains a set of tensed propositions that describe exactly how everything happens at specific moments of time that are subsequent to God's act of creating that universe. Second, the decree sets in place a particular set of tensed propositions that will change their truthvalues as history progresses. For example, prior to the act of creation, God's decree would settle the truthvalues for propositions like <God the Son will become incarnate>. Once God the Son becomes incarnate, that proposition will no longer be true. Instead, the tensed proposition <God the Son is incarnate> becomes true. Third, the decree seems to settle which emotions God will undergo, yet I am uncertain to what extent the decree can do so.[11] At the very least, the decree does not give God those experiences immediately.

Recall my earlier discussion on divine simulation. A cognitively perfect God will know the difference between what it is like to experience a simulation of an event, and what it is like to experience the actual event. Prior to creating a universe, God can simulate what it might be like to create a universe, but this is not the same kind of knowledge that one has of

10. Feinberg, *No One Like Him*, 801–2.
11. As several philosophers of emotion have told me, content essentialism for phenomenal knowledge is a controversial position.

actually creating a universe. God's decree to create a particular universe does not give God knowledge of what it is actually like to create a universe. Only creating a universe will give God such experiential knowledge. So why create? In order to gain the experiential knowledge of actually creating a universe. The same goes for God's knowledge of what will take place in history. God's decree only establishes that certain events will take place. This does not provide God with the experiential knowledge of what it is actually like to become incarnate, to respond to human prayers, to rejoice when humans repent, and so on. That kind of knowledge can only be had by actually creating a universe, and providentially interacting with it.

Given all of this, I think that this particular open theist objection is unsuccessful. However, there is another open theist objection worth considering. Open theists like Richard Rice and William Hasker argue that if God knows the future, then it makes no sense to speak of God having various emotions predicated of him in Scripture like anticipation, sadness, anger, grief, or happiness. One might even try to argue that foreknowledge calls into question the intelligibility of God's passibility as a whole. If Rice and Hasker are right, this is a problem for the theological determinist and the Molinist.

What exactly is the argument? According to Rice,

> The traditional view of divine foreknowledge collapses any distinction between anticipation and realization. According to the classical view, God's knowledge of the future is exhaustive: God knows the entire future, the future in all its detail. If so, then God not only knows exactly what will occur, God also knows every aspect of his own response to what will occur, and to know that, in effect, is to have the experience already. If God foreknows all, then God's experience already includes all. Actual occurrences contribute nothing new.[12]

I disagree with Rice's statement here. This ignores the distinction between propositional and phenomenal knowledge that most people want to make. God's foreknowledge is merely propositional. God can only experience what presently exists. Future events do not yet exist for God to experience. Nothing about knowing that God will respond to certain future events will give God knowledge of what it is like to actually respond. God can only have that experiential knowledge by actually experiencing the response when it happens. For example, God can know that he will respond to repentant sinners with joy. Nothing about foreknowing this response includes the actual experience of joy because those damned sinners have

---

12. Rice, *Future of Open Theism*, 135.

not yet repented. It would be irrational for God to already be experiencing joy when those wretches have yet to even ask for forgiveness. Since God is perfectly rational, his emotions will perfectly track the values in his present situation. God's present situation does not include all future events. God's present situation only includes all present events.

Hasker offers a different version of the argument. Hasker explicitly takes aim at anyone who wishes to affirm divine passibility and foreknowledge. His goal is to persuade the passibilist to affirm the open theistic view that God does not have definite exhaustive foreknowledge.[13] Hasker says,

> If, like me, you think God really does have an emotional life, then you may also feel you have some stake in being able to say that the emotions attributed to God in Scripture are emotions he really experiences. If that is what you want, the open view of God can give it to you—and so far as I can see, it is the only view that can.[14]

Hasker says that there are two characteristics to the biblical description of God's emotional life:

1) The emotion ascribed to God is concerned with, and appropriate to, the particular situation of the human beings to whom God is related.

2) The emotion would be profoundly different if we assumed it to be informed by a definite prior knowledge of the situation's outcome.[15]

As it stands, the argument is underdeveloped and does not seem to get Hasker to the conclusion that he wants. Remember, Hasker said that open theism is the only view that can maintain divine passibility. I do not see how (1) and (2) can lead to an incompatibility between divine foreknowledge and divine passibility. In what follows, I will offer several reasons for thinking that (1) and (2) cannot lead to any inconsistency between divine foreknowledge and divine passibility.

The first reason for thinking that there is no inconsistency is to recall the basic definitions of passibility and foreknowledge. Again, to be passible

---

13. Hasker, *Providence, Evil, and the Openness of God*, 105.

14. Hasker, *Providence, Evil, and the Openness of God*, 106. I can imagine some contemporary classical theists trying to dismiss this argument by asserting that it assumes a univocal theory of religious language. For some theologians, the doctrine of univocity is practically the same as worshiping the devil. Such a dismissal is mistaken for at least two reasons. First, Hasker affirms the doctrine of analogy, as do many open theists. See Hasker, "Reply to My Friendly Critics." Second, the doctrine of univocity is true and salutary. See Williams, "Doctrine of Univocity Is True and Salutary."

15. Hasker, *Providence, Evil, and the Openness of God*, 106.

is for God to have his beliefs, emotions, and actions influenced by things external to himself. God has foreknowledge if God knows of the truthvalues of the tensed propositions concerning the future. Say that God knows that you will repent of your sins and ask for forgiveness on January 8, 2025, at 2:17 p.m. Also, say that God knows that he will immediately offer forgiveness after you have successfully repented. Also, as the Bible tells us repeatedly, God will rejoice whenever a sinner repents. When that event arrives, God's belief that you are asking for repentance will be influenced by you presently asking for repentance. God's subsequent action of forgiving you will be influenced by your request for forgiveness. Finally, God's emotion of rejoice is justified by your actual present repentance. That is a passible deity through and through. Nothing about divine foreknowledge undermines passibility.

There are at least two more reasons for thinking that Hasker's argument cannot show the incompatibility of divine foreknowledge and divine passibility. First, (2) seems false. Second, (2) seems perfectly consistent with everyday passible creatures, so we have no reason to think that it is inconsistent with a divine passible being.

I will start with a reason for thinking that (2) is false. Pearson argues that emotions can be appropriate or inappropriate independent of the appropriate beliefs involved. The argument from Rice and Hasker seems to overlook this point. Pearson says,

> If I learn that a loved one will die on a particular date in the distant future, it is inappropriate for me to at that time to grieve the death. That is, it is inappropriate to have grief where the belief element involved is the belief "x will die at t" or the tenseless belief "x dies at t." Such grief would be inappropriate despite the belief it involves being true and appropriate.[16]

I find this statement plausible. Imagine that a psychic doctor helps deliver your first born child. The doctor hands you your baby and says to you, "I have seen the future. Your child will die in a hundred years." What kind of emotion will you have? I cannot really speak for you, but my guess is that grief will not be the emotion that arises. You might feel excited that your child will have a long life. You might be annoyed at the doctor for bringing up a far off death at this moment. Grieving the forthcoming death of your child in that situation seems inappropriate despite the fact that your belief about the child's death is true. This is because there are more salient tensed facts that ought to motivate you to have certain emotions. A far off death is not the most pressing tensed fact.

16. Pearson, *Rationality, Time, and Self*, 212–13.

Here is another example of this. In Matthew 9:14–17, several people notice that John's disciples and the Pharisees are fasting. Jesus's disciples are not fasting. This seems to have rankled these people, so they ask Jesus why his disciples are not fasting. Jesus says to them, "Can the wedding guests mourn as long as the bridegroom is with them? The days will come when the bridegroom is taken away from them, and then they will fast." Jesus knows that his death is forthcoming, yet he does not think that it is appropriate for his disciples to fast and mourn just yet. Why? Because there will be plenty of time to mourn later. At the moment, there are more pressing facts that should be motivating the disciples to have certain emotions and actions.

As I see it, (2) is just plain false in certain cases. Yet I also think that (2) is irrelevant to whether or not someone is passible. Again, emotions are justified by the present tensed facts. Some of the present tensed facts are about what will take place in the future. Merely knowing what will happen in the future will certainly temper my present emotions, but it in no way undermines the fact that I have emotions. Nor does it undermine the fact that I am a passible being. Basically, all (2) is doing is pointing out very common emotional experiences that all passible humans have.

Consider the classic example from A. N. Prior's "thank goodness that is over" argument for the tensed theory of time. Prior says that he is anxious about an upcoming exam. He knows that the exam *will* take place on Monday. And he knows that after the exam he *will* feel a great sense of relief. But knowing that he will eventually feel relief does not get rid of Prior's present anxiety. Why? Because it would be irrational to feel relief when the exam has not yet taken place. The present facts are that the exam is upcoming, and that justifies Prior's emotion of anxiety. You can probably say that Prior's anxiety is tempered by his knowledge that the exam will eventually finish, but that does not undermine his entirely justified anxiety.

Consider the case of Jesus Christ. He predicted that he would suffer and die on a cross and be raised three days later. The night before he was crucified, he prayed that the Father might spare him of this forthcoming crucifixion. Jesus has already stated that he will in fact be resurrected in three days, but for some reason this knowledge about what will happen in the future does not seem to get rid of his anxiety about his upcoming crucifixion. Why? Because Jesus's anxiety is an appropriate response to the present facts. The present facts are that he will be undergoing an immense suffering very soon. It would be irrational for Jesus to have an emotional response like "thank goodness that is over" when the crucifixion has yet to take place. To be sure, I guess one can say that Jesus's knowledge of his forthcoming resurrection tempered his anxiety in that moment. But Jesus still got so anxious that he sweat blood (Luke 22:44). If Jesus is justified in having emotional responses like that while still knowing something about the future, then I find myself unpersuaded that there is some deep conflict between passibility and foreknowledge.

Again, what all of these examples show is that we all have the very common experience of having our present emotions tempered by what we know will take place in the future. Nothing about this common experience of passible beings shows that foreknowledge is inconsistent with passibility.

Tyler McNabb and Michael DeVito offer a different take on the argument. They do not try to establish that foreknowledge and passibility are incompatible. They make a much weaker claim than Hasker and Rice. Their claim is that if God has exhaustive foreknowledge, then God does not seem to be as emotional as passibilists typically say.[17] Surely if God knows that he will have ultimate victory over sin, sickness, and death, then God's emotions should be sensitive to that knowledge.

I reply that God's emotions are sensitive to this knowledge, but that this is not news to the passibilist. The open theist Keith Ward has written on this in several places. He claims that there are certain emotions that God cannot fully grasp because he cannot experience them himself. As I mentioned in an earlier chapter, Ward gives the example of utter hopelessness. Ward claims that God can understand what it is like for you to feel utterly hopeless, but that God can never feel utter hopelessness himself. Why? Because God knows that his plan for creation will ultimately be successful.

McNabb and DeVito's point should be well taken. I don't think this is a particular problem for my view, but it should force certain passibilists to be more cautious with their language when describing God's emotional life. As I have pointed out earlier, I don't think one can get much traction out of predicating surprise of God. This will be surprising to some passibilists since they often make the emotion of surprise part of their argument for passibility. I think surprise arguments are surprisingly overstated. I think it is safe to say that God experiences a range of emotions from happiness, sadness, anger, and so on. But of course one should keep in mind that God knows his plan for the future. Nothing about this undermines the case for passibility. Again, passibility says that God can be moved or influenced by creatures for his beliefs, emotions, and actions. No amount of foreknowledge seems to change that.

Before closing, I suppose it is worth pointing out an oddity with theological determinism and passibility. I have alluded to the oddity before, but I want to make it explicit. Consider the emotion of divine wrath. Can God

---

17. DeVito and McNabb, "Foreknowledge and Divine Emotions."

really be rationally angry at you for sinning when he caused you to sin? That sounds like an irrational emotion. What about sadness? Can God be rationally sad at witnessing a tragic event when he caused that tragic event? Again, that sounds like an irrational emotion. As I see it, mere foreknowledge is not inconsistent with passibility, but theological determinism might be. It is difficult for me to figure out what to say about the emotional life of a Calvinist God. Since he causally determines everything, anger and sadness seem like odd emotions to have. Perhaps God has some kind of stoic resolve as he brings about various events in history. Perhaps one could argue that it would be rational for God to have some empathetic sadness for his creatures in their plight, but that stills seems off to me. My difficulty in figuring this out comes down to my difficulty in understanding how divine determinism is compatible with human freedom. If they are compatible, then the Calvinist can make all of the claims about divine emotion that one sees in the writings of Feinberg and Bruce Ware. But if divine determinism and human freedom are incompatible, then I am at a loss as to what the Calvinist should say about God's emotional life. Since I am not pursuing the compatibility or incompatibility of determinism and human freedom in this book, I should end this discussion for now. Any further discussion would be off topic.

Conclusion

It is time to draw this little book to a close. It has been quite the journey to get here, has it not? I am sure that many questions are still in your mind. You may even have various objections to my views. Odds are that I have dealt with the objections in other writings, and I invite you to explore those. One of my hopes with this book is that I have presented a God who can possibly care about you. I do not believe that the classical conception of God can possibly care about you which is why I prefer a biblical understanding of God. First Peter 5:7 tells us to cast our cares and concerns onto God because God cares for us. That is the kind of God to consider drawing close to.

I want to end this book by once again reflecting on what it means to be close to God. You are close to a person when you grasp their character, understand their cares and concerns, and learn how to support their projects. Throughout this book, I have given quite a bit of consideration to God's character, what God cares about, and what God's project is for creation. I have said that one of God's most central purposes for creation is to enter into friendship with humans. If you want to be close to God, you will want to promote God's project of friendship.

Some will object to my suggestion that we should promote or support God's project. For some, this will lead to the question, "Isn't it unthinkable to say that God needs our help to accomplish his goals?" I hear this kind of question a lot, but I ask you to notice something. I never said that God *needs* our help. Again, theologians seem to have forgotten the childhood lesson of the difference between needs and wants. My claim is this: God wants friendship with humans, and genuine friendship starts with our response to God's gracious offer. God has desired to create a world where humans contribute to his projects. Otherwise, why would God continually make his plan known to us, and call us to support his project of spreading the gospel? The biblical commands to God's people make no sense without the presupposition that God wants us to support his projects. So not only is it thinkable to say that God wants our help, it is the only thing that makes any sense of God's desire to enter into friendship with humanity.

I assume that if you have read this far in the book that you at least have some interest in knowing God well. Recall that there is a difference between knowing someone well and being in a close, personal relationship with that person. Since I don't know you personally, I cannot say if you want to be close to God. I cannot tell if you actually want to be friends with God. That is a deeply personal question that I cannot answer for you. It can even be a scary question to ask. "Do I really want to be close to God?" This question might seem like an obvious yes for some, but for others the question comes with a great deal of baggage. This is because the lives of some can be filled with suffering and tragedy that leads to a distrust of the creator of the universe. When trust has been broken either in appearance or in reality, it can be difficult to restore.

I believe that God understands this very well. God knows that he has asked a great deal from us when placing us in a universe like this. It is a marvellous universe filled with opportunities to cultivate truth, beauty, and goodness. Yet it is also a universe filled with opportunities to cultivate lies, ugliness, and wickedness. God knows of our predicament, and he has demonstrated that he is willing to endure the same plight as us by becoming incarnate in human flesh. God does not ask us to endure anything that he himself is unwilling to endure.

God is also patient with us, desiring that all shall come to him. The patience of an everlasting God is something to marvel at. Our patience often grows thin after fifteen minutes. Yet the eternal God does not count patience as we do. For us, a thousand years seems like a long time, but for God that is not too terribly long. God is willing to be patient with us in a way that boggles the mind, but fills me with hope for humanity. If you are unsure about whether or not to be friends with God, I understand. But know that God is more patient than you can fathom. He is willing to wait for you to make up your mind.

If you are unsure about whether or not to be friends with God, it might be because you find yourself with little faith. Fear not, for God can do much with the smallest seeds of faith. One only needs the most modest of faith to begin their friendship with God. All that is required is to believe that God exists, and that he does good for those who seek him (Heb 11:6). From there, the friendship can grow forever and ever. Amen.

Bibliography

Adams, Marilyn McCord. *Christ and Horrors: The Coherence of Christology.* Cambridge: Cambridge University Press, 2006.
———. *Horrendous Evils and the Goodness of God.* Ithaca, NY: Cornell University Press, 1999.
Amyraut, Moise. *Amyraut on Predestination.* Translated by Matthew Harding. Oswestry, UK: Charenton Reformed, 2017.
Anderson, James N. "Election, Grace, and Justice: Analyzing an Aporetic Tetrad." In *T&T Clark Handbook of Analytic Theology*, edited by James M. Arcadi and James T. Turner. London: T. & T. Clark, 2021.
Anselm. "Proslogion." In *Anselm of Canterbury: The Major Works*, edited by Brian Davies and G. R. Evans. New York: Oxford University Press, 2008.
Aquinas, Thomas. *Summa Contra Gentiles.* Translated by English Dominican Fathers. London: Burns, Oates, and Washbourne, 1934.
Arbour, Benjamin H. "A Few Worries About the Systematic Metaphysics of Open Future Open Theism." In *Philosophical Essays Against Open Theism*, edited by Benjamin H. Arbour. London: Routledge, 2019.
———. "Maximal Greatness and Perfect Knowledge." In *T&T Clark Handbook of Analytic Theology*, edited by James M. Arcadi and James T. Turner. London: T. & T. Clark, 2021.
Armstrong, D. M. *Truth and Truthmakers.* Cambridge: Cambridge University Press, 2004.
Augustine, Saint. *The Trinity.* Translated by Edmund Hill. Hyde Park, NY: New City Press, 1991.
Balslev, Anindita Niyogi. "Time and the Hindu Experience." In *Time and Religion*, edited by Anindita Niyogi Balslev and J. N. Mohanty. Leiden: Brill, 1992.
Bartley, C. J. *The Theology of Ramanuja: Realism and Religion.* London: Routledge, 2002.
Bates, William. *The Whole Works of the Rev. W. Bates.* Vol. 1. Edited by W. Farmer. Harrisonburg, VA: Sprinkle, 1999.
Berkhof, Louis. *Systematic Theology.* Edinburgh: The Banner of Truth Trust, 1984.
Betzler, Monika. "The Relational Value of Empathy." In *The Value of Empathy*, edited by Maria Baghramian et al. London: Routledge, 2021.
Bignon, Guillaume. "Lord Willing and God Forbid: Divine Permission, Asymmetry, and Counterfactuals." In *Calvinism and Middle Knowledge: A Conversation*, edited by John D. Laing et al. Eugene, OR: Pickwick, 2019.

Boethius. *The Trinity Is One God Not Three Gods*. Translated by H. F. Stewart. London: Putnam, 1918.

Bohn, Einar Duenger. *God and Abstract Objects*. Cambridge: Cambridge University Press, 2019.

Bonaventure. *The Works of Bonaventure: The Breviloquium II*. Translated by Jose de Vinck. New York: St. Anthony Guild Press, 1963.

Bossche, Frank Van Den. "Jain Arguments Against Nyaya Theism: A Translation of the Isvarotthapaka Section of Gunaratna's Tarka-Rahasya-Dipika." *Journal of Indian Philosophy* 26 (1998) 1–26.

Boyd, Gregory A. "God Limits His Control." In *Four Views on Divine Providence*, edited by Dennis W. Jowers. Grand Rapids, MI: Zondervan, 2011.

———. "The Open Future, Free Will and Divine Assurance: Responding to Three Common Objections to the Open View." *European Journal for Philosophy of Religion* 7 (2015) 207–22.

Brady, Michael S. *Emotional Insight: The Epistemic Role of Emotional Experience*. Oxford: Oxford University Press, 2013.

Brasnett, Bertrand R. *The Suffering of the Impassible God*. London: Macmillan, 1928.

Brito, Stephane A. De, et al. "Psychopathy." *Nature Reviews Disease Primers* 7 (2021) 1–21.

Broadie, Alexander. "Scotistic Metaphysics and Creation Ex Nihilo." In *Creation and the God of Abraham*, edited by David B. Burrell et al. Cambridge: Cambridge University Press, 2010.

Brunner, Emil. *The Christian Doctrine of Creation and Redemption*. Translated by Olive Wyon. London: Lutterworth, 1952.

Bulbulia, Joseph. "Bayes and the Evolution of Religious Beliefs." In *Debating Christian Theism*, edited by J. P. Moreland et al. Oxford: Oxford University Press, 2013.

Byerly, T. Ryan. *God Knows the Future by Ordering the Times*. Oxford Studies in Philosophy of Religion 5. Oxford: Oxford University Press, 2014.

———. *The Mechanics of Divine Foreknowledge and Providence: A Time-Ordering Account*. London: Bloomsbury Academic, 2014.

Calvin, John. *Institutes of the Christian Religion*. Translated by Henry Beveridge. Grand Rapids, MI: Eerdmans, 1989.

Cameron, Ross P. *The Moving Spotlight: An Essay on Time and Ontology*. Oxford: Oxford University Press, 2015.

Charnocke, Stephen. *Several Dischourses upon the Existence and Attributes of God*. London: Newman, 1682.

Clarke, Samuel. *A Demonstration of the Being and Attributes of God and Other Writings*. Cambridge: Cambridge University Press, 1998.

Clore, Gerald L. "Psychology and the Rationality of Emotion." *Modern Theology* 27 (2011) 325–38.

Collins, Robin. "The Teleological Argument: An Exploration of the Fine-Tuning of the Universe." In *The Blackwell Companion to Natural Theology*, edited by William Lane Craig and J. P. Moreland. Oxford: Blackwell, 2012.

Correia, Fabrice, and Sven Rosenkranz. *Nothing to Come: A Defence of the Growing Block Theory of Time*. Cham: Springer, 2018.

Couenhoven, Jesse. *Predestination: A Guide for the Perplexed*. London: T. & T. Clark, 2018.

Craig, William Lane. "The Molinist Response." In *God and the Problem of Evil: Five Views*, edited by Chad Meister and James K. Dew. Downers Grove, IL: InterVarsity, 2017.

———. "A Molinist View." In *God and the Problem of Evil: Five Views*, edited by Chad Meister and James K. Dew. Downers Grove, IL: InterVarsity, 2017.

———. "No Other Name: A Middle Knowledge Perspective on the Exclusivity of Salvation through Christ." *Faith and Philosophy* 6 (1989) 172–88.

———. *Time and Eternity: Exploring God's Relationship to Time*. Wheaton, IL: Crossway, 2001.

Crisp, Oliver D. *Analyzing Doctrine: Toward a Systematic Theology*. Waco, TX: Baylor University Press, 2019.

———. *Deviant Calvinism: Broadening Reformed Theology*. Minneapolis: Fortress, 2014.

Daeley, Justin J. "Divine Freedom and Contingency: An Intelligibility Problem for (Some) Theistic Compatibilists." *Religious Studies* 51 (2015) 563–82.

Damascus, John of. *Exposition of the Orthodox Faith*. In *A Select Library of the Nicene and Post-Nicene Fathers of the Christian Church*, vol. 9, edited by Philip Schaff and Henry Wace, translated by S. D. F. Salmond. Edinburgh: T. & T. Clark, 1898.

Davies, Brian. *The Reality of God and the Problem of Evil*. London: Continuum International, 2006.

Deonna, Julien A., and Fabrice Teroni. *The Emotions: A Philosophical Introduction*. New York: Routledge, 2012.

DeVito, Michael, and Tyler Dalton McNabb. "Foreknowledge and Divine Emotions: A Further Exploration into the Emotional Life of a Passible God." *European Journal for Philosophy of Religion* 14 (2022) 115–28.

Diamond, James A. "The Living God: On the Perfection of the Imperfect." In *The Question of God's Perfection: Jewish and Christian Essays on the God of the Bible and Talmud*, edited by Yoram Hazony and Dru Johnson. Boston: Brill, 2019.

Dolezal, James E. *All That Is In God: Evangelical Theology and the Challenge of Classical Christian Theism*. Grand Rapids, MI: Reformation Heritage, 2017.

———. "Strong Impassibility." In *Divine Impassibility: Four Views of God's Emotions and Suffering*, edited by Robert J. Matz and A. Chadwick Thornhill. Downers Grove, IL: IVP Academic, 2019.

Driel, Edwin Chr. van. *Incarnation Anyway: Arguments for Supralapsarian Christology*. New York: Oxford University Press, 2008.

Ekstrom, Laura W. "The Practical Life of God." In *Current Controversies in Philosophy of Religion*, edited by Paul Draper. New York: Routledge, 2019.

Erickson, Millard J. *Christian Theology*. 2nd. Grand Rapids, MI: Baker, 2004.

Evans, C. Stephen. *God and Moral Obligation*. Oxford: Oxford University Press, 2013.

Feinberg, John. *No One Like Him: The Doctrine of God*. Wheaton, IL: Crossway, 2001.

Fergusson, David. *Creation*. Grand Rapids, MI: Eerdmans, 2014.

Fiocco, Marcello Oreste. "What Is Time?" *Manuscrito* 40 (2017) 43–65.

Flint, Thomas P. *Divine Providence: The Molinist Account*. Ithaca, NY: Cornell University Press, 1998.

Florio, Ciro De, and Aldo Frigerio. *Divine Omniscience and Human Free Will: A Logical and Metaphysical Analysis*. Cham: Palgrave Macmillan, 2019.

Fretheim, Terence E. *The Suffering of God: An Old Testament Perspective*. Philadelphia: Fortress, 1984.

———. *What Kind of God? Collected Essays of Terence E. Fretheim*. Edited by Michael J. Chan and Brent A. Strawn. Winona Lake, IN: Eisenbrauns, 2015.

Frost, Gloria. "Three Competing Views of God's Causation of Creaturely Actions: Aquinas, Scotus, and Olivi." In *Philosopical Essays on Divine Causation*, edited by Gregory E. Ganssle. New York: Routledge, 2022.

Furlong, Peter. *The Challenges of Divine Determinism: A Philosophical Analysis*. Cambridge: Cambridge University Press, 2019.

Goris, Harm. "Divine Foreknowledge, Providence, Predestination, and Human Freedom." In *The Theology of Thomas Aquinas*, edited by Rik Van Nieuwenhove and Joseph Wawrykow. Notre Dame: University of Notre Dame Press, 2005.

Grant, W. Matthews. *Free Will and God's Universal Causality: The Dual Sources Account*. London: Bloomsbury Academic, 2019.

Greyson, Bruce. *After: A Doctor Explores What Near-Death Experiences Reveal about Life and Beyond*. London: Bantam, 2021.

Grim, Patrick. "Problems with Omniscience." In *Debating Christian Theism*, edited by J. P. Moreland et al. Oxford: Oxford University Press, 2013.

Grossl, Johannes, and Leigh Vicens. "Closing the Door on Limited-Risk Open Theism." *Faith and Philosophy* 31 (2014) 475–85.

Hardy, Edward R. *Christology of the Later Fathers*. London: Westminster, 1954.

Harvey, Ramon. *Transcendent God, Rational World: A Maturidi Theology*. Edinburgh: Edinburgh University Press, 2021.

Hasker, William. "An Adequate God." In *Searching for an Adequate God: A Dialogue Between Process and Free Will Theists*, edited by John B. Cobb Jr. and Clark H. Pinnock. Grand Rapids, MI: Eerdmans, 2000.

———. "Future Truth and Freedom." *International Journal for Philosophy of Religion*, forthcoming.

———. "A Non-Classical Alternative to Anselm." In *Philosophy of Religion: The Key Thinkers*, edited by Jeffrey J. Jordan. London: Continuum International, 2011.

———. "The (Non-) Existence of Molinist Counterfactuals." In *Molinism: The Contemporary Debate*, edited by Ken Perszyk. Oxford: Oxford University Press, 2011.

———. "An Open Theist Theodicy of Natural Evil." In *Molinism: The Contemporary Debate*, edited by Ken Perszyk. Oxford: Oxford University Press, 2011.

———. "An Open Theist View." In *God and the Problem of Evil: Five Views*, edited by Chad Meister and James K. Dew. Downers Grove, IL: IVP Academic, 2017.

———. *Providence, Evil and the Openness of God*. London: Routledge, 2004.

———. "Reply to My Friendly Critics." *Roczniki Filozoficzne* 70 (2022) 191–223.

Hazony, Yoram. "Is God 'Perfect Being'?" In *The Question of God's Perfection: Jewish and Christian Essays on the God of the Bible and Talmud*, edited by Yoram Hazony and Dru Johnson. Boston: Brill, 2019.

Helm, Bennett W. "Emotions and Practical Reason: Rethinking Evaluation and Motivation." *Nous* 35 (2001) 190–213.

———. "Emotions and Recalcitrance: Reevaluating the Perceptual Model." *Dialectica* 2015 (2015) 417–33.

Helm, Paul. "The Augustinian-Calvinist View." In *Divine Foreknowledge: Four Views*, edited by James K. Beilby and Paul R. Eddy. Downers Grove, IL: InterVarsity, 2001.

———. "Divine Timeless Eternity." In *God and Time: Four Views*, edited by Gregory E. Ganssle. Downers Grove, IL: InterVarsity, 2001.

———. *Eternal God: A Study of God Without Time*. 2nd ed. Oxford: Oxford University Press, 2010.

———. "Impossibility of Divine Passibility." In *The Power and Weakness of God*, edited by Nigel M. de S. Cameron. Edinburgh: Rutherford House, 1990.

———. "The 'Openness' in Compatibilism." In *Philosophical Essays Against Open Theism*, edited by Benjamin H. Arbour. London: Routledge, 2019.

———. *The Providence of God*. Downers Grove, IL: InterVarsity, 1993.

Helseth, Paul Kjoss. "God Causes All Things." In *Four Views on Divine Providence*, edited by Dennis W. Jowers. Grand Rapids, MI: Zondervan, 2011.

Hick, John H. *Evil and the Love of God*. London: MacMillan, 1977.

———. "An Irenaen Theodicy." In *Encountering Evil: Live Options in Theodicy*, edited by Stephen T. Davis. Edinburgh: T. & T. Clark, 1981.

Holtzen, Wm. Curtis. "Friends with Benefits." In *Partnering with God: Exploring Collaboration in Open and Relational Theology*, edited by Tim Reddish et al. Grasmere, ID: SacraSage, 2021.

Howard-Snyder, Frances. "Divine Freedom." *Topoi* 36 (2017) 651–56.

Inwagen, Peter van. "What Does an Omniscient Being Know about the Future?" In *Oxford Studies in Philosophy of Religion*, edited by Jonathan L. Kvanvig. Oxford: Oxford University Press, 2008.

Jorati, Julia. "Leibniz on Divine Causation: Continuous Creation and Concurrence Without Occasionalism." In *Philosophical Essays on Divine Causation*, edited by Gregory E. Ganssle. New York: Routledge, 2022.

Judisch, Neal. "Meticulous Providence and Gratuitous Evil." *Oxford Studies in Philosophy of Religion 4*. Oxford: Oxford University Press, 2012.

Kierland, Brian, and Bradley Monton. "Presentism and the Objection from Being-Supervenience." *Australasian Journal of Philosophy* 85 (2007) 485–97.

Kittle, Simon. "Against Synchronic Free Will: Or, Why a Personal, Free God Must Be Temporal." In *The Divine Nature: Personal and A-Personal Perspectives*, edited by Simon Kittle and Georg Gasser. London: Routledge, 2022.

Koperski, Jeffrey. *The Physics of Theism: God, Physics, and the Philosophy of Science*. Malden, MA: Wiley Blackwell, 2015.

Kraay, Klaas J., ed. *God and the Multiverse: Scientific, Philosophical, and Theological Perspectives*. London: Routledge, 2015.

———. "Theism, Possible Worlds, and the Multiverse." *Philosophical Studies* 147 (2010) 355–68.

Kretzmann, Norman. "A General Problem of Creation: Why Would God Create Anything at All?" In *Being and Goodness: The Concepts of the Good in Metaphysics and Philosophical Theology*, edited by Scott MacDonald. London: Cornell University Press, 1991.

———. "A Particular Problem of Creation: Why Would God Create This World?" In *Being and Goodness: The Concepts of the Good in Metaphysics and Philosophical Theology*, edited by Scott MacDonald. London: Cornell University Press, 1991.

Kronen, John, and Eric Reitan. *God's Final Victory: A Comparative Philosophical Case for Universalism*. New York: Continuum International, 2011.

Kvanvig, Jonathan L. *Depicting Deity: A Metatheological Approach*. Oxford: Oxford University Press, 2021.

Lamb, David T. *The Emotions of God: Making Sense of a God Who Hates, Weeps, and Loves*. Downers Grove, IL: InterVarsity, 2022.

Lebens, Samuel. *The Principles of Judaism*. Oxford: Oxford University Press, 2020.
Leftow, Brian. *God and Necessity*. Oxford: Oxford University Press, 2012.
———. "Infinite Goodness." In *The Infinity of God: New Perspectives in Theology and Philosophy*, edited by Benedikt Paul Göcke and Christian Tapp. Notre Dame: University of Notre Dame Press, 2019.
———. "Perfect Being Theology and Friendship." In *The Question of God's Perfection: Jewish and Christian Essays on the God of the Bible and the Talmud*, edited by Yoram Hazony and Dru Johnson. Boston: Brill, 2019.
———. "Why Perfect Being Theology?" *International Journal for Philosophy of Religion* 69 (2011) 103–18.
Leslie, John. "A Way of Picturing God." In *Alternative Concepts of God: Essays on the Metaphysics of the Divine*, edited by Andrei A. Buckareff and Yujin Nagasawa. New York: Oxford University Press, 2016.
Lombard, Peter. *The Sentences Book 1: The Mystery of the Trinity*. Translated by Giulio Silano. Ontario: Pontifical Institute of Mediaeval Studies, 2007.
Lucas, J. R. *A Treatise on Time and Space*. London: Clowes, 1973.
Lukasiewicz, Darius. "On William Hasker's Theodicy, the Doctrine of Continuous Creation, and the Nature of Morality." *Roczniki Filozoficzne* 70 (2022) 155–71.
MacGregor, Kirk R. *Molinist Philosophical and Theological Ventures*. Eugene, OR: Pickwick, 2022.
Maimonides, Moses. *The Guide for the Perplexed*. Translated by M. Friedländer. New York: Dover, 1956.
Marschler, Thomas. "Substantiality and Personality in the Scholastic Doctrine of God." In *Rethinking the Concept of a Personal God: Classical Theism, Personal Theism, and Alternative Concepts of God*, edited by Thomas Schärtl et al. Munster: Aschendorff Verlag GMBH & Co. KG, 2016.
Martin, Nicholas. "Simplicity's Deficiency: Al-Ghazali's Defense of the Divine Attributes amd Contemporary Trinitarian Metaphysics." *Topoi* 36 (2017) 665–73.
Mawson, T. J. *The Divine Attributes*. Cambridge: Cambridge University Press, 2018.
———. "Divine Free Will." In *The Routledge Companion to Free Will*, edited by Kevin Timpe et al. London: Routledge, 2017.
———. "Omnipotence and Necessary Moral Perfection Are Compatible: A Reply to Morriston." *Religious Studies* 38 (2002) 215–23.
McCann, Hugh J. *Creation and the Sovereignty of God*. Bloomington: Indiana University Press, 2012.
———. "Free Will and the Mythology of Causation." In *Alternative Concepts of God: Essays on the Metaphysics of the Divine*, edited by Andrei A. Buckareff and Yujin Nagasawa. New York: Oxford University Press, 2016.
McCann, Hugh J., and Jonathan L. Kvanvig. "The Occasionalist Proselytizer: A Modified Catechism." *Philosophical Perspectives* 5 (1991) 587–615.
McConnell, Francis J. *The Christlike God: A Survey of the Divine Attributes from the Christian Point of View*. New York: The Abingdon Press, 1927.
———. *The Divine Immanence*. New York: Methodist Book Concern, 1906.
———. *Is God Limited?* London: Williams and Norgate, 1924.
McIntosh, C. A. "Why Does God Exist?" *Religious Studies* (forthcoming) 1–22.
Melamed, Yitzhak Y. Introduction to *Eternity: A History*, edited by Yitzhak Y. Melamed. Oxford: Oxford University Press, 2016.
Merricks, Trenton. "The Only Way to Be." *Nous* 53 (2019) 593–612.

---. "Truth and Molinism." In *Molinism: The Contemporary Debate*, edited by Ken Perszyk. Oxford: Oxford University Press, 2011.
---. *Truth and Ontology*. Oxford: Oxford University Press, 2007.
Meyer, Ulrich. *The Nature of Time*. Oxford: Oxford University Press, 2013.
Molina, Luis De. *On Divine Foreknowledge: Part IV of the Concordia*. Translated by Alfred J. Freddoso. Ithaca, NY: Cornell University Press, 1988.
Moberly, R. W. L. *Old Testament Theology: Reading the Hebrew Bible as Christian Scripture*. Grand Rapids, MI: Baker Academic, 2013.
Morris, Thomas V. *Our Idea of God: An Introduction to Philosophical Theology*. Downers Grove, IL: InterVarsity, 1991.
Morton, Adam. "Empathy and Imagination." In *The Routledge Handbook of Philosophy of Empathy*, edited by Heidi L. Maibom. London: Routledge, 2017.
Mozley, J. K. *The Impassibility of God: A Survey of Christian Thought*. Cambridge: Cambridge University Press, 1926.
Muller, Richard A. *Divine Will and Human Choice: Freedom, Contingency, and Necessity in Early Modern Reformed Thought*. Grand Rapids, MI: Baker Academic, 2017.
Mullins, R. T. "Closeness with God: A Problem with Divine Impassibility." *Journal of Analytic Theology* 10 (2022) 233–45.
---. "The Creator/Creature Distinction in Debates over Models of God." *Religions* 13 (2022) 1–16.
---. "Divine Temporality and Providential Bodgery." *TheoLogica* 5 (2021) 147–74.
---. "Divine Temporality, the Trinity, and the Charge of Arianism." *Journal of Analytic Theology* 4 (2016) 267–90.
---. *The End of the Timeless God*. Oxford: Oxford University Press, 2016.
---. *God and Emotion*. Cambridge: Cambridge University Press, 2020.
---. "Identity through Time and Personal Salvation." In *Being Saved: Explorations in Human Salvation*, edited by Marc Cortez et al. London: SCM, 2018.
---. "The Philosophy of Eternal Life." In *Deconstructing Hell: Open and Relational Responses to the Doctrine of Eternal Conscious Torment*. Grasmere, ID: SacraSage, 2023.
---. "The Problem of Arbitrary Creation for Impassibility." *Open Theology* 6 (2020) 392–406.
---. "Simply Impossible: A Case Against Divine Simplicity." *Journal of Reformed Theology* 7 (2013) 181–203.
---. "Why Can't the Impassible God Suffer?" *TheoLogica* 2 (2018) 3–22.
Mullins, R. T., and Shannon Byrd. "Divine Simplicity and Modal Collapse: A Persistent Problem." *European Journal for Philosophy of Religion* 14 (2022) 21–51.
Mullins, R. T., and Emanuela Sani. "Open Theism and Risk Management: A Philosophical and Biological Perspective." *Zygon* 56 (2021) 591–613.
Murphy, Mark C. *God's Own Ethics: Norms of Divine Agency and the Argument from Evil*. Oxford: Oxford University Press, 2017.
---. "Is an Absolutely Perfect Being Morally Perfect?" In *Current Controversies in Philosophy of Religion*, edited by Paul Draper. New York: Routledge, 2019.
Murray, Michael J., and Jeffrey P. Schloss. "Evolutionary Accounts of Religion and the Justification of Religious Belief." In *Debating Christian Theism*, edited by J. P. Moreland et al. Oxford: Oxford University Press, 2013.
Nagasawa, Yujin. *Maximal God: A New Defense of Perfect Being Theism*. Oxford: Oxford University Press, 2017.

Nemes, Steven. *Theological Authority in the Church: Reconsidering Traditionalism and Hierarchy.* Eugene, OR: Cascade, 2022.

O'Connor, Timothy. "The Unity of the Divine Nature: Four Theories." In *Classical Theism: New Essays on the Metaphysics of God*, edited by Jonathan Fuqua and Robert C. Koons. London: Routledge, 2023.

Oord, Thomas Jay. *Pluriform Love: An Open and Relational Theology of Well-Being.* Grasmere, ID: SacraSage, 2022.

———, ed. *Theologies of Creation: Creatio Ex Nihilo and Its New Rivals.* New York: Routledge, 2015.

Pearson, Olley. *Rationality, Time, and Self.* Cham: Palgrave Macmillan, 2018.

Peckham, John C. *Divine Attributes: Knowing the Covenantal God of Scripture.* Grand Rapids, MI: Baker Academic, 2021.

———. *The Doctrine of God: Introducing the Big Questions.* London: T. & T. Clark, 2020.

———. *The Love of God: A Canonical Model.* Downers Grove, IL: IVP Academic, 2015.

———. "Qualified Passibility." In *Divine Impassibility: Four Views of God's Emotions and Suffering*, edited by Robert J. Matz and A. Chadwick Thornhill. Downers Grove, IL: IVP Academic, 2019.

———. *Theodicy of Love: Cosmic Conflict and the Problem of Evil.* Grand Rapids, MI: Baker Academic, 2018.

Pereboom, Derk. "Libertarianism and Theological Determinism." In *Free Will and Theism: Connections, Contingencies, and Concerns*, edited by Kevin Timpe and Daniel Speak. Oxford: Oxford University Press, 2016.

———. "Theological Determinism and the Relationship with God." In *Free Will and Classical Theism: The Significance of Freedom in Perfect Being Theology*, edited by Hugh J. McCann. Oxford: Oxford University Press, 2017.

Perrett, Roy W. *An Introduction to Indian Philosophy.* Cambridge: Cambridge University Press, 2016.

Pink, Arthur W. *The Attributes of God.* Grand Rapids, MI: Baker, 1975.

Plantinga, Alvin. *God, Freedom, and Evil.* Grand Rapids, MI: Eerdmans, 1974.

———. *The Nature of Necessity.* Oxford: Clarendon, 1974.

———. *Warranted Christian Belief.* Oxford: Oxford University Press, 2000.

Pruss, Alexander R. "Divine Creative Freedom." In *Oxford Studies in Philosophy of Religion*, edited by Jonathan L. Kvanvig. Oxford: Oxford University Press, 2017.

Rasmussen, Joshua. "Could God Fail to Exist?" *European Journal for Philosophy of Religion* 8 (2016) 159–77.

Rea, Michael. *Metaphysics: The Basics.* New York: Routledge, 2014.

Renard, John, ed. *Islamic Theological Themes: A Primary Source Reader.* Oakland: University of California Press, 2014.

Rhoda, Alan R. "The Fivefold Openness of the Future." In *God in an Open Universe: Science, Metaphysics, and Open Theism*, edited by William Hasker et al. Eugene, OR: Pickwick, 2011.

———. "Open Theism and Other Models of Divine Providence." In *Models of God and Alternative Ultimate Realities*, edited by Jeanine Diller and Asa Kasher. New York: Springer, 2013.

Rice, Richard. *The Future of Open Theism: From Antecedents to Opportunities.* Downers Grove, IL: IVP Academic, 2020.

Roberts, Robert C. *Emotions in the Moral Life.* Cambridge: Cambridge University Press, 2013.

Rogers, Katherin A. "Foreknowledge, Freedom, and Vicious Circles: Anselm vs Open Theism." In *Philosophical Essays Against Open Theism*, edited by Benjamin H. Arbour. London: Routledge, 2019.

Rowe, William, ed. *God and the Problem of Evil.* Malden: Blackwell, 2001.

Sanders, John. *The God Who Risks: A Theology of Divine Providence.* Downers Grove, IL: IVP Academic, 2007.

Schultz, Walter J. *Jonathan Edwards' "Concerning the End for Which God Created the World": Exposition, Analysis, and Philosophical Implications.* Gottingen: Vandenhoeck & Ruprecht, 2020.

Scrutton, Anastasia. *Thinking Through Feeling: God, Emotion and Passibility.* New York: Continuum International, 2011.

Shedd, W. G. T. *Dogmatic Theology.* Vol. 1. New York: Scribner, 1888.

Smart, Ninian. *Doctrine and Argument in Indian Philosophy.* New York: Humanities Press, 1964.

Soteriou, Matthew. "The Ontology of Emotion." In *The Ontology of Emotions*, edited by Hichem Naar and Fabrice Teroni. Cambridge: Cambridge University Press, 2018.

Speaks, Jeff. *The Greatest Possible Being.* Oxford: Oxford University Press, 2018.

Strong, Augustus Hopkins. *Systematic Theology.* Volume 1, *The Doctrine of God.* Philadelphia: American Baptist Publication Society, 1907.

———. *Systematic Theology.* Volume 2, *The Doctrine of Man.* Philadelphia: American Baptist Publication Society, 1907.

Swinburne, Richard. *The Christian God.* Oxford: Oxford University Press, 1994.

———. *The Coherence of Theism.* Oxford: Oxford University Press, 2016.

———. *The Existence of God.* Oxford: Oxford University Press, 2004.

———. *Providence and the Problem of Evil.* Oxford: Oxford University Press, 1998.

Taliaferro, Charles. *Consciousness and the Mind of God.* Cambridge: Cambridge University Press, 1994.

Tallant, Jonathan. *Truth and the World: An Explanationist Theory.* London: Routledge, 2018.

Tappolet, Christine. "The Metaphysics of Moods." In *The Ontology of Emotions*, edited by Hichem Naar and Fabrice Teroni. Cambridge: Cambridge University Press, 2018.

Thomas, Emily. *Absolute Time: Rifts in Early Modern British Metaphysics.* Oxford: Oxford University Press, 2018.

Tiessen, Terrance L. "A Response to John Laing's Criticisms of Hypothetical-Knowledge Calvinism." In *Calvinism and Middle Knowledge: A Conversation*, edited by John D. Laing et al. Eugene, OR: Pickwick, 2019.

Timpe, Kevin. *Free Will in Philosophical Theology.* London: Bloomsbury Academic, 2014.

Todd, Cain. "Emotion and Value." *Philosophy Compass* 9 (2014) 702–12.

Todd, Patrick. *The Open Future: Why Future Contingents Are All False.* Oxford: Oxford University Press, 2021.

Turner, James T. *On the Resurrection of the Dead: A New Metaphysics of Afterlife for Christian Thought.* London: Routledge, 2019.

Turretin, Francis. *Institutes of Elenctic Theology.* Vol. 1. Phillipsburg: Presbyterian and Reformed, 1992.

Tuttle, Jacob. "Durand and Suarez on Divine Causation." In *Philosophical Essays on Divine Causation*, edited by Gregory E. Ganssle. New York: Routledge, 2022.

Vicens, Leigh, and Simon Kittle. *God and Human Freedom*. Cambridge: Cambridge University Press, 2019.

Visala, Aku. "Human Cognition and the Image of God." In *The Christian Doctrine of Humanity: Explorations in Constructive Dogmatics*, edited by Oliver D. Crisp and Fred Sanders. Grand Rapids, MI: Zondervan, 2018.

Ward, Keith. *Christ and the Cosmos: A Reformulation of Trinitarian Doctrine*. Cambridge: Cambridge University Press, 2015.

———. *The Christian Idea of God: A Philosophical Foundation for Faith*. Cambridge: Cambridge University Press, 2017.

———. "Cosmos and Kenosis." In *The Works of Love: Creation as Kenosis*, edited by John Polkinghorne. Grand Rapids, MI: Eerdmans, 2001.

———. *Religion and Creation*. Oxford: Oxford University Press, 1996.

Ward, Thomas M. *Divine Ideas*. Cambridge: Cambridge University Press, 2020.

Webster, John. "On the Theology of Providence." In *The Providence of God*, edited by Francesca Aran Murphy and Philip G. Ziegler. London: T. & T. Clark, 2009.

Wessling, Jordan. *Love Divine: A Systematic Account of God's Love for Humanity*. Oxford: Oxford University Press, 2020.

White, Nicholas. *A Brief History of Happiness*. Oxford: Blackwell, 2006.

Wierenga, Edward R. *The Nature of God: An Inquiry into Divine Attributes*. Ithaca, NY: Cornell University Press, 1989.

Wiertz, Oliver. "Classical Theism." In *Rethinking the Concept of a Personal God: Classical Theism, Personal Theism, and Alternative Concepts of God*, edited by Thomas Schartl et al. Munster: Aschendorff Verlag, 2016.

Williams, Thomas. "The Doctrine of Univocity Is True and Salutary." *Modern Theology* 21 (2005) 575–85.

Zagzebski, Linda. *Omnisubjectivity: A Defense of a Divine Attribute*. Milwaukee, WI: Marquette University Press, 2013.

———. "Omnisubjectivity: Why It Is a Divine Attribute." *Nova et Vetera* 14 (2016) 435–50.

Zimmerman, Dean. "The A-Theory of Time, Presentism, and Open Theism." In *Science and Religion in Dialogue*, edited by Melville Y. Stewart. Malden: Blackwell, 2010.

Made in the USA
Monee, IL
26 November 2024